PERFORMANCE-DRIVEN GIVING

Endorsements for Performance-Driven Giving

The only financial advice my mom ever gave me was to be wildly generous. My first instruction was to tithe 10 percent of my gross income back to the local church. This advice has served me well. David Hancock and Bobby Kipper take this advice a step further in his book *Performance-Driven Giving*. If we are going to be wildly successful, we must unleash this powerful tool called generosity.

—**Aaron T. Walker**, founder of View from the Top, life
and business coach, and author of *View from the Top*

So much of today's society is built upon selfish inquiries and investments. However, I choose to believe that many crave to serve from the heart. David Hancock and Bobby Kipper streamline what giving looks like and how you can connect your desire to perform with your will to perform. Get ready to look beyond what you see and experience how to turn an upside-down world right side up with *Performance-Driven Giving*.

—**Kristianne Wargo**, international bestselling author, podcaster,
and founder of Create Your Now, LLC

Do you want to be a legendary leader? If so, *Performance-Driven Giving* is required reading to not only live a legendary life, but help everyone around you do so as well.

—**Tommy Breedlove**, *Wall Street Journal* and *USA Today*
national bestselling author of *Legendary*

I love the challenge and reminders that David Hancock and Bobby Kipper lay out in *Performance-Driven Giving* for small business owners like myself. It is easy to forget that we are all stewards of what God has graciously given to us and, as such, we have a responsibility to steward it well. As a leader, I am thankful for the reminder that we have the privilege to give voluntarily and with joy, if we so choose. If you are an entrepreneur or small business owner, as I am, and desire to build a team and culture that grows together in their giving, I can't recommend *Performance-Driven Giving* enough. Never underestimate the power of that first small gift.

—**Victoria Mininger**, CEO/integrator, Bear Creek Outdoor Living

Performance-Driven Giving is a refreshingly readable trove of ideas and tactics on the deeply misunderstood concept of giving. Follow even a small fraction of its guidance and you will enjoy a significantly more enriching life.

—**Bea Boccalandro**, author of *Do Good at Work: How Simple Acts of Social Purpose Drive Success and Wellbeing* and corporate purpose advisor

The principles in *Performance-Driven Giving* will help you make a difference in people's lives—not just today, but for future generations. Generosity is key, and this book is a vital resource for every leader.

—**Chris Niemeyer**, investor and entrepreneur, REInvest Capital Group

Business success, that's what we all want. We work on strategy, vision, leadership, and financial history and forecasting and think that is enough. But without the power of giving, the impact we could have on our communities and society is diminished. *Performance-Driven Giving* will show you the way, with clear-cut, actionable steps to building this essential habit. The rewards will be exponential not only in business, but also in life.

—**Christine Odle**, CEO/CFO of Rockin' Beeby Enterprises, LLC, and author of *Rockin' Your Business Finances* and *The Adventures of Black Goat and Yellow Dog*

You can read all the books on personal growth and leadership, but without the power of giving, you'll fall short of your potential. *Performance-Driven Giving* is the key to help you unlock your potential and perform at the highest levels.

—**Jeff McManus**, Chief Cultivation Officer, The Jeff McManus Group, and author of *Growing Weeders into Leaders*

Giving is the foundation for a successful life, no matter what your role or position. David Hancock and Bobby Kipper share their wisdom as entrepreneurs and leaders to ensure you have the tools to make a massive difference in the world.

—**Kim Avery**, certified business coach and author of *The Prayer Powered Entrepreneur: 31 Days to Building Your Business with Less Stress and More Joy*

Performance-Driven Giving is an insightful guide that gives you clear steps to build a habit that can change your family, organization, and ultimately the world. Get it today!

—**Nick Pavlidis**, founder and CEO of Authority Ghostwriting and Ghostwriter School

Performance-Driven Giving is, in itself, a gift! It provides a 360° perspective on giving. It asks the hard questions and provides concrete suggestions for self-assessment and methods for change. It draws upon the experiences and wisdom of successful leaders, and is grounded in biblical examples that light the path for all of us. You would find it difficult to locate a more complete discussion of the personal and organizational motivations for, impediments to, and rewards for giving. This is definitely an inspirational read!

—**Rita Ralston**, executive director at Ronald McDonald House Charities of Charlottesville, Inc.

Finally, a framework we can wrap our hearts and minds around…literally! The HEART framework in *Performance-Driven Giving* is the perfect guide for those who know they should be giving but struggle with putting the principles of giving into practice. Well done!

—**Paul Klein**, co-founder/producer @BizableTV and business consultant

Performance-Driven Giving should be required reading for every coach, consultant, and leader who wants to harness the power of giving to make a massive difference in people's lives.

—**Teresa McCloy**, coach and creator of the REALIFE Process˚

What terrific inspiration for growing a giving mindset. Not only can *Performance-Driven Giving* bear fruit one hundred years from now, but it can also foster fulfillment for the giver today!

I highly recommend digging into this timeless resource.

—**Mark Ross**, encorepreneur, executive coach, and artist

David and Bobby understand this greatest secret of high achievers: that the more you give, the greater you become. *Performance-Driven Giving* will show you how to cultivate the spirit of generosity, put it into everyday practice, and unleash its extraordinary power to make your life greater. Don't miss this priceless book!

—**John David Mann**, coauthor of the million-selling classic *The Go-Giver*

The most successful business leaders and entrepreneurs know that the power of giving increases their potential for impact. This powerful book will help you grow and lead in ways you never thought possible. David Hancock and Bobby Kipper have given us a real gem!

—**Skip Prichard**, president & CEO, OCLC, Inc., author of the
Wall Street Journal bestseller *The Book of Mistakes:
9 Secrets to Creating a Successful Future*

Performance-Driven Giving is a lifestyle that fuses performance-driven thinking and giving to serve others at the highest level. It's a means to create win-win opportunities where everyone benefits. *Performance-Driven Giving* enhances everyone's life, plus creates ripples that reach new people for weeks, months, and decades into the future. This book shares a step-by-step approach to implement performance-driving giving into all aspects of your everyday life. This book will help you take lifelong journey that builds lasting legacies.

—**Charles George**, entrepreneur, publisher, direct marketer at Publish to Thrive

Giving is in the heart and habits of every great leader I have known. *Performance-Driven Giving* has impacted me and influenced me to be more intentional with my giving, and as you read and apply the principles, you will be too. David and Bobby are great men that emulate the spirit of giving as an example to each of us. Let's become great leaders by being great givers.

—**Gregory Gray**, author of *Business Owner Freedom* and host of the *Everyday Business Leader* podcast

Giving is the best thing you can do for yourself. This book helps you understand why and how. As a leadership coach, I'm using *Performance-Driven Giving* as a guiding light for serving my clients. These pages contain priceless truths that can change your life and transform the lives of your clients, teams and the world around you.

—**Marianne Renner**, leadership coach and keynote speaker

As someone who has spent my career in public service, I can attest that giving makes a difference, no matter what the context. *Performance-Driven Giving* will help every leader understand the importance of giving and how to implement it in your business or organization.

—**Janet V. Green**, CEO of Habitat for Humanity
Peninsula and Greater Williamsburg, Virginia

Everyone has the power to help others by giving. *Performance-Driven Giving* will give you the practical tools to change your mindset, impact your organization or business, and build a habit than impacts future generations. Don't miss this powerful book!

—**Ryan Steuer**, founder of Leading for Legacy

Some well-meaning people intend to be generous, and others live a generous lifestyle. In *Performance-Driven Giving,* David Hancock and Bobby Kipper share biblical principles, practical guidelines, and inspiring testimonies to help readers go from good intentions to consistent actions. It truly is more blessed to give than to receive. David and Bobby are great guides because they themselves are practitioners. Join them on this journey, and watch how your life and those around you are impacted.

—**Les Hughes**, pastor, author, podcaster, co-founder of EntrePastors

PERFORMANCE DRIVEN GIVING™

THE ROADMAP TO UNLEASHING THE POWER OF GENEROSITY IN YOUR LIFE

DAVID L. HANCOCK
BOBBY KIPPER
WITH KENT SANDERS

NEW YORK

LONDON • NASHVILLE • MELBOURNE • VANCOUVER

Performance-Driven Giving

The Roadmap to Unleashing the Power of Generosity in Your Life

Published in New York, New York, by Morgan James Publishing. Morgan James is a trademark of Morgan James, LLC. www.MorganJamesPublishing.com

Proudly distributed by Ingram Publisher Services.

Scripture quotations are from The ESV® Bible (The Holy Bible, English Standard Version®), copyright © 2001 by Crossway, a publishing ministry of Good News Publishers. Used by permission. All rights reserved.

Morgan James BOGO™

A **FREE** ebook edition is available for you or a friend with the purchase of this print book.

CLEARLY SIGN YOUR NAME ABOVE

Instructions to claim your free ebook edition:
1. Visit MorganJamesBOGO.com
2. Sign your name CLEARLY in the space above
3. Complete the form and submit a photo of this entire page
4. You or your friend can download the ebook to your preferred device

ISBN 9781631957246 paperback
ISBN 9781631957253 ebook
Library of Congress Control Number:
2021914731

Cover & Interior Design by:
Christopher Kirk
www.GFSstudio.com

Morgan James is a proud partner of Habitat for Humanity Peninsula and Greater Williamsburg. Partners in building since 2006.

Get involved today! Visit MorganJamesPublishing.com/giving-back

CONTENTS

An Important Notice

Before you start reading, make sure to download the *Performance-Driven Giving* supplementary material from the website. You will get access to the full interviews of the people featured in the book, plus additional bonuses that will enhance your performance driven journey.

Download the supplementary material at:
PerformanceDrivenThinking.com/Giving

Also, we would love to hear from you. We would enjoy hearing your thoughts, ideas, and inspiration on how the book impacted you and your life. Please, share your story at:
PerformanceDrivenThinking.com/Story

PART 1
Establishing Your Roots

CHAPTER 1

The Seeds of Greatness

We make a living by what we get, we make a life by what we give.
—Sir Winston Churchill

One of the most beloved films of all time is Frank Capra's *It's a Wonderful Life*. Jimmy Stewart plays George Bailey, a local banker who always wanted to escape his life in the small town of Bedford Falls. While all his classmates were off living exciting lives, he stayed stuck in his humdrum life. George believes his life is a failure because he never accomplished big things.

One day his uncle Billy loses $8,000 in cash. This sends George into a tailspin. Things keep getting worse until, finally, he decides the only way out is to take his own life. Before he can go through with it, Clarence the angel rescues him. Then he shows George what life would have been like for the people of Bedford Falls if he had never been born.

The ending of *It's a Wonderful Life* shows the whole community coming to support George in his time of need. He is overwhelmed by their generosity. Near the end of the film, George holds up a book from Clarence that magically appears on the pile of money. The inscription reads, "No man is a failure who has friends."

This heartwarming story has inspired generations of movie lovers. Why? Because it reminds us of an important truth: Giving is the best way to live. This is what our parents taught us as children. As kids, we heard phrases like "'Tis better to give than receive" or "Sharing is caring." Everyone knows that it's better to be a giver like George Bailey than a selfish old man like Mr. Potter.

If we all love givers and see the value of living this way, why do we have such a crisis of giving in the world today?

Perhaps as adults, we become desensitized to the needs of the world around us. As we grow up and move out of our parents' homes, we get consumed with our own needs. We have jobs, houses, families, and other commitments. Many people find themselves being crushed under the weight of consumer debt, not to mention the college graduates who face mountains of debt from student loans.

In this context of entitlement and "me first," it's easy to get consumed with material goods and put our full focus on making as much money as possible. We become cynical and selfish, only concerned about ourselves and what we can gain from others. While money can certainly be helpful, it's not the be all, end all of our existence. But we sometimes act like we are competing with others to get the most toys at the end of the game.

Although we all admire givers, few of us actually want to become one. So again, we ask: If we value giving so much, why are so few people actually givers? What are the benefits of giving? How do we create a culture of giving within our families, businesses, and, ultimately, the world?

Those are some of the questions we set out to answer in this follow-up to the first volume in the Performance Driven series: the *Wall Street Journal* and *USA Today* bestselling book *Performance Driven Thinking*™. In that book, we looked at the vital role thinking plays in driving our performance. We showed how your thinking impacts your performance in every area of your life. If you want to be successful, it begins with good thinking.

In this book, we want to take the next natural step in the performance-driven process: giving. This may seem like an unusual step, but we'll show why true success is not only about yourself and how you perform—it's about how giving benefits everyone around you and ultimately helps you to perform better. We aim to show how giving can help you become a better parent, team member, and leader.

One of the most pressing questions on the minds of people today is "How do I measure success?" Perhaps that's always been the case throughout history. However, it's especially vital today since there are so many different ways to become financially successful. That being said, money is not the ultimate measurement of success.

Many of the world's most financially successful people agree. As Jay Conrad Levinson and Jeannie Levinson wrote in *The Best of Guerrilla Marketing: Guerrilla Marketing Remix*, "Of all the pitfalls, the money morass is the deepest, darkest, and biggest. As lack of money is toxic to human existence, too much money can be equally toxic. That's why entrepreneurs like John D. Rockefeller and Bill Gates spent the first half of their lives accumulating money and the second half giving it away."

That is a great perspective on true success. It's not about accumulation—it's about impacting others through giving and leaving the world a better place than you found it.

In the rest of this book, we'll dive into various aspects of giving and show how giving can impact every area of your life. But first, let's take a look at the concept of performance-driven giving and why it's so important.

What Is Performance-Driven Giving?

In *Performance-Driven Thinking*, we wrote, "we realized that performance didn't depend solely on the desire to succeed, and it didn't solely depend on the effort or will to succeed. The two needed to be connected through a particular thought process. We have defined this process as Performance-Driven Thinking, and we think it could change your life!" We went on to define performance-driven thinking as "The thought process that connects the *desire* to perform with the *will* to perform a specific task or goal."

We are more committed than ever to the performance-driven framework! How, then, does giving tie into the performance that drivers your thinking?

Giving is a natural outgrowth of performance-driven thinking. It takes it to the next level because the most successful people recognize that we are all interconnected in a web of relationships, whether it's family, church, school, business, or community. The best performers are those who know it's not about them—it's about how much they can give and serve others.

In other words, performance-driven giving takes the concepts we taught in the previous book and shows how good thinking naturally progresses into giving within every area of your life.

Our definition of performance-driven giving flows directly from the thinking process we outlined in the previous book:

> ## Performance-Driven Giving
> The giving process that connects the *desire* to perform with the *will* to perform a specific task or goal.
> **Desire:** To long or hope for something we want.
> **Will:** To decide, attempt, or bring desire to action.

Throughout this book, we aim to show you how giving is the next logical step to take if you want to connect your desire to perform with your will to perform.

We also want to emphasize that giving is ultimately an action that you take. Many intend to give, or would like to give, but they don't end up taking action. We want you to think of giving as an action that is part of your everyday life. Performance-driven thinking can have a radical impact on your life, but if you want to take it even further, you can implement it even better by giving.

Five Convictions about Giving

As we begin our journey into performance-driven giving, let's take a moment to reflect on five core convictions that drive our perspective on giving.

1. Giving begins with you.

As you read this book, you'll be tempted to think about your family, friends, or co-workers who need to hear what we have to say. And yes, they do! We would love for as many people as possible to hear our message about giving.

But remember, it begins with you. We all have to start somewhere, and many people have not been taught basic principles about giving. Change begins with you and your personal giving.

2. The most powerful giving is based in community.

There are many ways to give as an individual: You can give money, time, encouragement, referrals, inspiration, and so many other things. But when you pair your giving with other people in your community, it's so much more powerful, whether it happens in your family, business, church, or other area.

It's the principle of synergy: When two or more people come together for a common goal, the whole is greater than the sum of its parts. There is creative, emotional, and financial power in community.

3. Giving impacts every area of your life.

One of the core differentiators between high achievers and average achievers is their understanding of how giving makes them greater. They understand the power of generosity and putting other people first. They know it's not possible to achieve anything worthwhile alone, and that we are built for community.

High achievers who are also great givers also know that giving helps them perform better because of the principle of reciprocity. When we give to others, they are inclined to give back. We can literally create value from nothing when we choose to give first, and then it is reciprocated in some way.

In the process, we make ourselves better. That is not the primary purpose of giving, but it's a natural result.

4. Most people want to give but don't know why or how.

If you look at the state of our "me first" culture today, you might be shocked to learn that anyone would want to give. It seems that everyone is entitled and only wants to accumulate power, wealth, and status for their own pleasure and security. However, that is a cynical view of the human spirit.

We believe that most people, deep down inside, truly want to give. But because of too much debt, endless distractions, too much despair, and frequent doubt, they face a lot of obstacles on their journey to becoming great givers.

Just as we said in the previous book that we are born to perform, we also believe that we are born to give. Giving is a learned habit, and one that children as well as adults can learn. However, they must be taught, and that process does not happen overnight.

5. Giving is the best way to leave a legacy.

There is a poignant scene near the end of the musical *Hamilton* when Aaron Burr fires a fatal shot at Alexander Hamilton. Time freezes in Alexander's mind as he observes that a legacy is like planting seeds you will never get to see come to fruition. That is the perfect way to view a legacy—something you are creating here and now, something that can impact people for generations to come.

Some people believe that a legacy means being famous. But fame has nothing to do with a legacy. You can be a famous artist or author, and millions of people may admire your work. But that doesn't mean your legacy was everything it could have been.

There are so many great legacies you've never heard of—people who have lived great lives and built great companies and organizations, who quietly helped untold numbers of people in big and small ways.

You don't have to be famous to create a legacy. You only have to be intentional. That's why we'll return again and again in this book to the metaphor of trees to help you become strong in your giving so you can impact many people over generations.

Givers are like sturdy oaks that stand the test of time. Non-givers are like tiny saplings that topple over in the wind. We want to help you plant the seeds of success in your life through giving, so you can in turn plant seeds that help others grow.

Where We're Coming From

We don't want you to think this is all talk. In our respective positions over the years, we have worked hard to put performance-driven giving into practice. But we don't speak as experts on this topic. We speak as fellow learners on the journey of continual giving. As such, we are excited to share our background on the topic of giving and why it is so important to us.

David's Story

One of the most vital aspects of our business at Morgan James is our work with the charitable organization Habitat for Humanity. Since 2006, we have been a proud partner of Habitat for Humanity Peninsula and

Greater Williamsburg. We place the Habitat logo on the back and inside of our books along with a statement of our passion for the organization.

We are honored to help raise awareness and donate books to the organization's life-changing work, which helps low-income families build decent homes they can afford to buy.

People sometimes ask me (David) why I'm so passionate about our involvement with Habitat. I always answer that it simply makes sense to me. One of the most basic human needs is having a place to live. Helping people achieve this goal is a way we can help a great organization and provide a foundational element in people's lives.

I have always been a fan of home ownership. I bought my first house when I was twenty years old. In my early days I was a real estate developer, and later a mortgage broker, so I saw firsthand the importance of putting people into a home. I chose Habitat for Humanity as a partner not only because they were meeting an important need, but also because they were nationally known. I knew it was a cause that would unite people.

Morgan James began helping Habitat by supporting the construction of a house every year, donating books, and speaking at Habitat events. We could also see where our money was going, which meant that our authors and others within the Morgan James sphere of influence could also see we were directly impacting lives.

In the early days of Morgan James, nobody knew who we were. The independent bookstores were the only ones giving us a chance. Although we weren't on their radar screen, and neither were some of our authors at the time, they saw us building houses down the street from their bookstore and supporting their communities. We weren't actually building the houses, but we were supporting the cause that was building a house near their store.

Many wonderful things happened because of our involvement with Habitat. For example, we were invited to ring the opening bell of NASDAQ in December 2008 because we were giving back to the public. The partnership between Morgan James Publishing and Habitat for Humanity has been a rich and rewarding experience from the very beginning.

Bobby's Story

I (Bobby) have always believed that the measure of a man is not what you get, but rather what you give. I have held this philosophy all throughout my career in both the private and public sectors. After serving twenty-six years with the police department in Newport News, Virginia, I was asked to join the attorney general's office in Virginia, where I served four years as the director of the Gang Reduction Program.

When we inherited $2.5 million of federal funding to reduce violence in the city of Richmond, I believed it should be used to serve the providers in the community. I have always believed that community comes first. Basically, I took a page out of the old Reaganomics playbook that says that if you grow a community and you shrink the role of government, you will be successful. And I still maintain that today.

When community is front and center, it has a positive effect on every other facet of life. We proved this in Richmond where we reduced crime 35 percent in eighteen months because we deployed resources to forty-four community partners, including eleven faith-based partners, to make sure that they were making a difference within their community.

My desire to give back culminated with the founding of the National Center for Prevention of Community Violence, which serves communities and schools across America in an effort to interrupt the process of violence through proven solutions. I believed that if the equation was working in the city of Richmond, why couldn't it work everywhere? This became a national model and the reason I wrote my first book for Morgan James Publishing, *No COLORS: 100 Ways to Stop Gangs from Taking Away Our Communities*. Many of the one hundred action steps featured in the book cost little or nothing.

Speaking of Morgan James, I'd like to share a quick story that not only illustrates my relationship with David Hancock—it's also a powerful story about giving.

My mood was down, and my future was not defined. I had completed a successful thirty-year public safety career with a number of local and national awards. Professionally, I was at a crossroads with my future and not sure where the next journey would take me. My situation was also impacted by a failed twenty-two-year marriage and the breakup of my family. For the first time in my life, I had more questions than answers.

I did not know David Hancock at this point, but I was introduced to him through a mutual friend. I met David one afternoon in a conference room in Hampton, Virginia. We were meeting to discuss the possibility of Morgan James publishing my first book, *No Colors*. Little did I know that this man would not only give this first-time author a chance, but he would also embrace a partially broken and drifting individual. He later become my dear friend and coach for the next phase of my life.

When I met David I wondered, *What makes David Hancock different?* I later discovered it was his spirit. You cannot help but feel it when you are in his presence. It is not just a feeling you get from David. It is witnessing his constant giving to others. Through his time, energy, and resources, David is one of the most giving men I have ever met. He is a unique example of what one person can do to positively influence the lives of others.

David gave me a renewed hope of understanding that life is not about what you have; it is about what you give. It's not just about money. The art of giving starts with the attitude of wanting to make a difference.

To say that David made a difference in my life is an understatement. He has coached me to never be satisfied with just getting by. His example is all about giving your best to others so they will shine.

He has been by my side since we started our national nonprofit to prevent violence—an organization that has impacted communities across

America. He has allowed us to become a leading voice to a broken world. David Hancock is the example of performance-driven giving.

By the way, this one-time high school remedial English student has gone on to write six books published by Morgan James. One of them became a *Wall Street Journal* and *USA Today* bestseller—the first book in the Performance Driven series, *Performance-Driven Thinking* (co-authored by David).

This relationship continues to grow and impact individuals both nationally and internationally. Just when you think David has given more than enough, he has pledged to give away thousands of free copies of my latest book, *Roll Call: Spiritual Wellness for Today's Law Enforcement Officer* (also published by Morgan James). Due to the giving spirit of my best friend and personal and professional performance coach, David Hancock, thousands of police officers will receive this life-changing book.

I am so grateful for the opportunity to co-author this book with David Hancock. He is truly performance-driven giving in action.

We hope this gives you a glimpse into our backgrounds and how we have tried to live out the principle of giving, in addition to being greatly impacted by the giving of others.

The Secret to Having More

As we come to the end of this chapter, stop for a moment to think about the state of your life, your family, and your organization. Maybe things are going well and you feel blessed beyond measure. Maybe you feel discouraged, stuck on a hamster wheel, and don't know how to get off. Or maybe you're just plain ready to quit.

No matter where you are in life and business, chances are good that you want more. You want more security, more freedom, more opportunities, more influence, more…everything! But how do you get more?

Here is the secret: it all begins with your thinking. Let's return to the definition of performance-driven thinking: "The thought process that connects the *desire* to perform with the *will* to perform a specific task or goal." In other words, your thinking is what causes you to take action to achieve great results.

The legendary broadcaster Earl Nightingale echoed this idea in his influential broadcast called *The Strangest Secret* when he said, "You become what you think about." If you want to have more, you must first become something more. Your thoughts literally change your life. We hope and expect that what you'll learn in *Performance-Driven Giving*™ will not only give you the knowledge to make a difference with giving, but help you take action as well.

Shel Silverstein's classic children's book *The Giving Tree* is a powerful story of generosity. The tree measured its success by how much it gave, not how much it took. The book's message runs counter to the conventional wisdom about success, which says we must take, take, take. But truly successful people are givers. In fact, givers are also the highest performers!

Are you ready to begin a life-transforming journey of giving?

Keys to Performance-Driven Giving

In order to sow the seeds of greatness in your life, consider the following:

1. Consider all the areas of your life that giving could impact. How could it positively affect your health, relationships, finances, personal development, career, and children?
2. Make a list of the opportunities you have been given. Think about your social circle, your work, your family, and your community. What are specific ways you can begin giving in those areas?
3. Who are the people in your life who have helped you get to where you are? Remember that no man is an island. We've all had help. Take a few moments to make a list and feel grateful for their impact.

Performance-Driven Giving: Answering the Objections

Everyone wants to be successful. However, there are certain topics related to success that are more sensitive than others. Giving is one of those topics. We know that even bringing up the topic will produce some pushback.

We thought it would be helpful to address many of the objections to giving here at the beginning of our journey.

I can't afford to give.

We have two responses to this. First, everyone can afford to give something. No matter how little you believe you have, you have something that you can give, and we will show you how. When it comes to giving, you are only limited by your imagination.

Second, we also believe that you cannot afford not to give. As you will see in the rest of this book, giving is one of the major keys that unlocks a life of blessing, abundance, and joy.

Giving is a nice idea, but it doesn't help me in everyday life.

Many people believe giving is a concept that is nice in theory but doesn't actually work in the real world. But when you give intentionally, especially to the people in your everyday life, you'll see amazing results that have a strong and immediate impact on your relationships in every area of your success.

You can be highly successful without giving.

Many people point to examples such as Steve Jobs, who achieved an extraordinary level of success while famously refusing to give to charity. Our responses that the exception proves the rule. Whenever you see people who are financially successful, the majority of the time they are givers and in one form or another.

On top of that, many successful people give in ways that you will never know. The very nature of giving is that much of it is done in secret, away from the eyes of the public.

We would also add, what was someone like Steve Jobs missing because he did not give? Imagine what greater success he could have achieved by being more intentional with his giving.

People around me don't give.

You may have heard the illustration of the crab basket. It goes like this: Whenever there is a basket full of crabs, and one tries to crawl out, the other crabs pull it back down. They cannot stand the thought of one of their own escaping, even if it means certain doom for them all.

Everyone wants to fit into their social situation. It is hard to grow and to become a giver when those around you are not. But don't let the lack of giving around you stop you from a life of blessing. Whenever you begin to elevate your life by giving, you can reach down and elevate others as well.

Nobody has given to me.

When we challenge others to give, we sometimes hear this sentiment: Why should I give when no one has given to me first? If you feel this way, we would challenge your thinking on that. No one has led a life where they have done things completely on their own. We have all benefited from the help of others in big and small ways.

It is not a matter of people not helping us; it is that we are not able to recount all the ways people have helped us.

And even if it were possible that no one has ever helped you, is that a reason to avoid giving to others? You can create a new cycle of giving even if you feel you were held back by others not giving to you.

My giving doesn't make any difference.

When you start to embrace a life of giving, it can feel like it doesn't make much difference. In the book of Mark, Jesus told a fascinating story about a widow who came into the temple and gave two small coins while others were giving much more. She was praised because even though she had given a small amount, to her it represented much. Therefore, she actually gave more than those who gave a much larger amount.

Never underestimate the power of your giving, no matter how small it may feel.

I don't know where to start.

My friend, that is why you are here! This book is all about practical action steps to help you get started and grow your giving over time. As they say, the journey of a thousand miles begins with a single step. And here at the end of this chapter, you've taken your first step. We are so proud!

A Conversation with Dan Miller, Business and Career Coach

We began this book by exploring a simple yet profound question: "How do I measure success?" As you've seen in this first chapter, one of the most important ways to measure success is through the lens of giving.

For our first interview, we are excited to feature our friend Dan Miller, one of the most generous and successful entrepreneurs we know. Dan is a career and business coach, as well as the author of an amazing book that has impacted countless lives: *48 Days to the Work and Life You Love.*

Dan is also the host of the wildly successful *48 Days* podcast, which helps people find or create work they love. As an authority on work, career, and business startups, he has a unique and helpful point of view on living a purposeful life and running a profitable business.

Dan is a big fan of setting goals, so we began this conversation by asking him about the connection between generosity and goals.

Yes, there certainly is a connection. I encourage people to develop goals in seven different areas: financial, social, family, physical, personal development, spiritual, and career. Those can all have the spirit of generosity or the spirit of stinginess and greed. It all comes down to your thinking about scarcity or abundance.

If we believe wealth is limited, then we see someone down the street who has a lot of money, we immediately think of ourselves as having less. If we assume that wealth is like a pie where there's only so much to go around, we will feel resentful when someone seems to have a bigger piece.

But that's not how money works. We create money out of nothing. And if you have a whole lot of money, I can learn from you and grow my own wealth. Not by taking your wealth away from you, but by learning the principles that helped you along the way.

Having an intentional goal-setting process, where we are pouring into every area of our lives, can keep us from this misguided kind of thinking.

One of the most fascinating aspects of the giving process is that some people who love to give don't feel comfortable with receiving. We wanted to find out why that is the case, and how Dan stays open to receiving gifts and generosity from others.

I'm so glad you are including that concept here because that's a really important part of this. It's the other side of the equation. If you're a generous giver, you need to learn to receive well.

That can be a very humbling experience. Many years ago, Joanne and I were on the receiving end where things had gone awry in a business. We were hundreds of thousands of dollars in debt, and we had to learn how to receive. But because we'd been generous prior to that, we had an outpouring of generosity that came back to us, and we experienced that side of it.

It is a personal skill to be developed, to learn how to receive well. Typically, people who don't receive well have a low sense of self-confidence.

We hear stories of people going through Starbucks and the person ahead of them paid for their order, and then it goes down the line and twelve more people have done that. That is all wonderful, but what if I don't pay for the person behind me? Does that make me greedy or ungrateful?

What if I just know how to receive without having to even the score? So many people want to immediately return the favor, or even get rid of it, when they receive a gift. They don't take responsibility for just having been a receiver.

So it really is something to be learned and a very positive, personal characteristic to be a gracious receiver.

Our final question to Dan focused on the kind of legacy he wants to leave through his work and giving.

Here is one of the funny things about where I am at this stage in my life. I'm seventy-three years old and just moved to Florida. People assume that I'm going there to retire.

That's the thing to do, right? Retire. That just makes my skin crawl. I don't know how to process the idea of not being productive. I may have enough money for myself, so I don't have to do anything, but that idea is mortifying.

> *I love the idea of being a good steward. This means that if God has given me the ability to produce income, I have the obligation to continue doing that. Not just for my own needs, but like the Old Testament says, blessed to be a blessing where it can flow through me to others.*
>
> *So as long as I have the ability to make money, I need to keep doing that. The point is not to get a bigger house or a fancier car, but to be able to funnel that in ways which are productive, ways that can assist other people.*

Thank you, Dan! We are so grateful for all the ways you have taught and inspired people to use their God-given gifts to serve others and create value.

Dan's website is 48days.com. Make sure to check out his amazing book, *48 Days to the Life and Work You Love*, which gives you fresh tips on job searching to bypass the competition, how to nail the interview, how to negotiate a higher salary, how to start your own business, and more. To listen to the entire interview, go to PerformanceDrivenThinking.com/Giving or scan the QR code to visit the page.

We also recommend connecting with Dan on social media:

Facebook: https://www.facebook.com/dan.miller.1829405
LinkedIn: https://www.linkedin.com/in/48days
Twitter: https://twitter.com/48DaysTeam
Podcast: https://www.48days.com/listen

CHAPTER 2

A Spiritual Perspective on Giving

*I have always found more joy in giving
when I did not expect anything in return.*
—S. Truett Cathy

Imagine that it's time for your annual eye exam. You make the appointment and clear your schedule, knowing that you'll be able to see more clearly once you get a new pair of glasses. When you visit the eye doctor, you go through the careful process of having an examination. You do the eye test, have those funny-looking eyepieces put in front of your eyes, and even the glaucoma test where they blow a puff of air in your eyes.

When the test is through, the eye doctor determines that you need a new prescription. You pay the bill and they tell you to come back the following week to pick up your new glasses. When you go back, the doctor opens the case for the new glasses and asks you to try them on to make sure everything is correct.

However, when you do that, you have the surprise of your life: The view is blurry and you can't see a thing. You have mistakenly been giving the wrong prescription, and your vision is all messed up!

That's where most people find themselves when it comes to the topic of giving. They need a new vision and a clearer perspective. But it's not their fault. They are only seeing the world through the glasses they have been given. We are here to help you see the issue of giving more clearly than ever before.

In this chapter, we will examine the critical issue of a spiritual perspective on giving. This is a sensitive and personal topic for many people. Sometimes things get uncomfortable when you start talking about God or the Bible as it relates to giving. Many people feel an overwhelming sense of guilt or shame because they don't give at all, or they don't give very much. Or perhaps they feel angry and irritated because all their church ever talks about is money.

Whatever your emotional state when it comes to this issue, we ask you to set that aside and hear us out. We'd like to help you gain a spiritual perspective on this issue. The reality is that we are eternal beings who need to hold an eternal perspective on giving. The giving you do during your brief lifetime here on earth has the potential to impact people for generations after you are gone.

Don't think of this chapter as a sermon to make you feel guilty. When we examine God's word for instructions about giving, we should feel liberated because it shows the pathway to greater impact and fulfillment.

Before we look at specific principles from God, it will be helpful to clear up two common misunderstandings about God and money.

The Two Misunderstandings

We want you to have the right "glasses" on so you can see giving from a correct perspective. Let's briefly examine two common misunderstandings around the issue of money. When these are cleared up, we can gain a clear perspective that allows us to see spiritual truth about money more clearly.

1. We misunderstand what money is.

All our lives, we have been taught to value money. We know we need it. We know we want it. And often we don't know how to get more of it! The bottom line is that we have a lot of stress and anxiety surrounding money, which only makes our misunderstanding worse.

At its core, money is stored energy. It is simply a medium of exchange that represents value one party has given to another for goods or services, or as a gift. The energy that is contained in money can make things happen, just like a battery in a flashlight. The stored energy contained in money has power.

Money is a means, not an end. Money has no value in itself. It only has value when it is used for something. It can give you options, it can purchase things, it can feed the poor, it can build houses, or it can cause all kinds of harm to others.

Money is neither good nor evil, but it causes good or evil things to happen. When it comes down to it, money is simply a tool, a container for energy or power that can be directed any way you choose.

2. We misunderstand where money comes from.

Remember your first job? Perhaps it was in high school or college. After you worked those first couple of weeks, you were so excited to get paid for the first time. And when you did, you probably felt like most young people do: You earned some money that you could now call your own! There was a sense of pride and ownership that you had earned money through your own hard work. And you were likely reluctant to share it with anyone.

But where did that money come from? Sure, it came from your employer, and ultimately it came from their customers or clients. But what is the true source of money? Where does it all come from?

We believe the ultimate source is God himself. As the Creator of the universe, God set time, space, and all of creation in motion. And because

He is the creator, that means He is ultimately the owner of everything that exists.

We don't use the word "steward" very often in our everyday talk, but it's a helpful concept to understand our true relationship with money. A steward is a caretaker or manager who is responsible for the well-being of another person's possessions or estate. Because God owns everything, we are simply stewards—or managers—of what He has entrusted to us.

That's why churches often refer to their campaigns to raise funds as "stewardship" campaigns. They are trying to help the people in their church use their funds to honor God and achieve their church's mission.

Some people think the concept of stewardship locks you in. "If it's all God's money, I can't do anything fun with it!" But that's not the case at all. Instead, stewardship is a concept that gives you immense freedom. When you realize that everything belongs to God anyway, you can relax because you now have an element of faith in your giving and finances.

How do we put these two concepts together? What do the concepts of energy and stewardship have to do with each other?

When we look at money through these twin lenses, we come to understand money in a new way: *money is God-given energy*. God has given us the privilege and responsibility of using the immense power of money for good in the world. We don't own the power—God owns it. He simply lets us use it for His glory and the good of the world.

In the last chapter, we defined performance-driven giving as "the giving process that connects the *desire* to perform with the *will* to perform a specific task or goal." This God-given energy—money—connects our desire and our will. In other words, it makes things happen. It's like electricity that can kill you or power your house. It all comes down to how you use it.

Now that we have a grounded understanding of what money is and where it comes from, let's look to God's word for some practical teaching on the purpose of the money God has entrusted to us.

Ten Principles of Giving

The most complete teaching on giving we have in the Bible is 2 Corinthians chapters 8–9. In these two chapters, the apostle Paul lays out an example of how Christ followers should live. One of those areas, of course, is giving.

It helps to have a bit of context for Paul's teaching here. He writes to the believers in the Greek city of Corinth in the hope they will complete the collection they had started earlier for the poor Christians in Jerusalem.

From this passage, we can draw ten principles for giving that are still relevant for us today. Although his words were written nearly two thousand years ago, Paul's words will help you live and give in a way that honors people and lifts you to a higher level of success, no matter what your faith background.

1. Giving is only made possible by God's grace.

*We want you to know, brothers, about the grace of God
that has been given among the churches of Macedonia…*
(2 Cor. 8:1–2)

Paul begins his encouragement of the Corinthians by reminding them of the example of the Macedonian believers who gave generously. But the act of giving did not truly begin with them—it began with God's grace. Without grace and the means to give, they would have never been able to follow through.

When you think of giving, why are so many people reluctant to do it? It's because they have a scarcity mindset. They believe there is only so much to go around. If they give their money, time, or resources to others, they will have less for themselves. They see their giving as beginning with them and their resources.

We reference again what we mentioned earlier: God owns everything. We are simply managers, or stewards, of what He has given us by His grace. This is not a limiting concept—it's a freeing one! When we realize that God owns everything, we are free to become channels of his grace to others (more on that later).

2. Giving draws out the best in us.

For in a severe test of affliction, their abundance of joy
and their extreme poverty have overflowed
in a wealth of generosity on their part.
(2 Cor. 8:2)

Trials and difficult situations can make you bitter or better. Difficulties are the great separator because it's only then that you discover what people are made of. You immediately see whether their attitude, inner strength, and mindset can help them use their problems as advantages to help them move forward or shrink back.

In his book *The Obstacle Is the Way*, Ryan Holiday writes, "This is one thing all great men and women of history have in common. Like oxygen to a fire, obstacles became fuel for a blaze that was their ambition. Nothing could stop them, they were (and continue to be) impossible to discourage or contain. Every impediment only served to make the inferno within them burn with greater ferocity."

The Macedonian Christians certainly embodied this principle. They rose to the occasion and used their difficult situation as a springboard for helping others. Zig Ziglar famously said, "You can have everything in life you want if you will just help enough other people get what they want." When we put others first, we improve ourselves and are blessed in the process.

3. Giving is a privilege.

For they gave according to their means, as I can testify,
and beyond their means, of their own accord, begging us
earnestly for the favor of taking part in the relief of the saints
—and this, not as we expected, but they gave themselves
first to the Lord and then by the will of God to us.
(2 Cor. 8:3–5)

The believers did not reluctantly give. They literally begged Paul for the opportunity to participate. They viewed it as a "favor" Paul was doing for them.

When is the last time you saw someone beg for the chance to help others? Have you ever heard anyone refer to giving as a favor someone was allowing them to do? It's virtually unheard of in today's world. That's why Paul's principles here are so relevant—they have fallen out of favor in today's me-focused world. It's time for a radical change in how we view giving and generosity.

John D. Rockefeller said, "Think of giving not as a duty but as a privilege." It is indeed a privilege—a unique pathway that allows God's grace to flow through us and help us grow in ways we cannot experience any other way. That is why Paul quoted the words of Jesus in Acts 20:35 when he said, "It is more blessed to give than to receive." It is also what makes giving such a privilege.

When is the last time you begged someone for the privilege of giving to them?

4. Giving is just as important as knowledge.

But as you excel in everything—in faith, in speech,
in knowledge, in all earnestness, and in our love for you
—see that you excel in this act of grace also.
(2 Cor. 8:7)

Have you ever hired someone at your organization or worked in an HR department? You probably made a list of important qualities you were looking for in a candidate. You were likely looking for someone who was qualified, presented themselves well, and had the skills and knowledge for the position. We are willing to bet that "giving" was not on your list of key qualities you were looking for.

However, Paul lists giving as a quality that is just as important as other character traits such as faith, speech, knowledge, and earnestness. In our Western culture, we place a high value on knowledge and education. Although there is less emphasis on the importance of a college education than there used to be, formal education is still a highly valued quality in most professional fields.

Perhaps we tend to overemphasize formal knowledge and undervalue a generous and giving spirit. As you look around at the people in your organization—and yourself as well—do you value giving as much as other key areas of success?

5. Giving is proof of your love for others.

I say this not as a command, but to prove by the earnestness of
others that your love also is genuine. For you know the grace of our
Lord Jesus Christ, that though he was rich, yet for your sake he
became poor, so that you by his poverty might become rich.
(2 Cor. 8:8–9)

Have you ever paid for an item in a retail store with a $100 bill? If so, you have likely seen a cashier hold the bill up to the light to make sure it is genuine. American currency has several features that are built into the money to assure merchants that it is genuine and help prevent counterfeiting.

In the same way, we should also periodically check ourselves to ensure that our love is genuine. Love for people is the reason we give. Giving is ultimately an issue of the heart. Do we love the people who are the recipients of our gifts? Do we care about them? Do we want the best for them? If so, then we will give.

That's not to say a person cannot give with a cold, uncaring heart. That is certainly the case. Individuals and companies do it all the time. It's possible to give because you want to get noticed or receive the good PR that comes from giving. Those might be results, but they should not be the reason. Love for people is the only reason to give. Paul shares the example of Jesus, who gave everything had—his life—because he loved people.

6. Giving should be voluntary without expecting anything in return.

> *So I thought it necessary to urge the brothers to go on ahead to you and arrange in advance for the gift you have promised, so that it may be ready as a willing gift, not as an exaction.*
> *(2 Cor. 9:5)*

Remember as a kid when your mom forced you to clean your room? You probably went through with it, but you hated the fact that you were forced to do it under threat of punishment. You also likely did the bare minimum of work required, putting in as little effort as possible to meet the requirements.

That is the complete opposite of how giving should work. Giving should always be completely voluntary. When giving is forced, or when people are motivated to give out of guilt, they will only do what is required and nothing more. Their hearts will not be in it.

Paul also says that our giving should not be an "exaction," a term that implies the giver is expecting something in return. When we give to others, we do so freely and should not expect the other party to reciprocate. It is a response to God's grace within our lives, not because we are driven out of guilt or compulsion.

This is a great principle for leaders to remember. It reminds us that God is the one who prompts our hearts to give. We can create opportunities, but we cannot force people.

7. We are blessed in accordance with our giving.

> *The point is this: whoever sows sparingly will also reap sparingly,*
> *and whoever sows bountifully will also reap bountifully.*
> *(2 Cor. 9:6)*

We have to be careful with this principle. Paul is not saying you will receive back exactly what you have given. He uses the language of farming and reminds us that we reap what we sow.

We can see this principle throughout the Bible. A few hundred years before the birth of Christ, the spiritual leaders of Israel were not giving properly to God. The prophet Malachi challenged them: "Bring the full tithes into the storehouse, that there may be food in my house. And thereby put me to the test, says the LORD of hosts, if I will not open the windows of heaven for you and pour down for you a blessing until there is no more need" (Malachi 3:10–12).

Likewise, Proverbs 11:24–25 says, "One gives freely, yet grows all the richer; another withholds what he should give, and only suffers want. Whoever brings blessing will be enriched, and one who waters will himself be watered."

God reminds us that whatever we give will come back to us in some way. He even challenged Israel's leaders to test Him! We cannot predict all the ways we will be blessed as a result of giving. However, we can be assured that it will return to us. In the end, we reap what we sow.

8. Our giving should be joyful.

> *Each one must give as he has decided in his heart, not reluctantly or under compulsion, for God loves a cheerful giver. And God is able to make all grace abound to you, so that having all sufficiency in all things at all times, you may abound in every good work.*
> *(2 Cor. 9:7–8)*

This is a great time to examine whether you feel joy whenever you give. If you do not, why? The reason is probably because you feel something is being taken away from you. You feel that something is now lacking.

But when we look at the principles we have discussed so far in the book, we know that God is the source of our blessing. He literally owns everything, so we don't need to worry about our needs not being supplied.

This does not mean that we give carelessly or without thought. It doesn't mean we should empty our bank accounts and give all our money away while we have obligations such as a mortgage, employee salaries, or health insurance. It simply means that if we practice responsible giving, we should feel joy because we are doing the right thing and adding value to our little corner of the world.

9. We are channels of God's blessing.

> *He who supplies seed to the sower and bread for food will supply and multiply your seed for sowing and increase the harvest of your*

*righteousness. You will be enriched in every way to be generous in
every way, which through us will produce thanksgiving to God.*
(2 Cor. 9:10–11)

Paul says that God is not only the supplier of the seed, but the one who
increases the harvest as well. In a sense, we are not ultimately responsible to
either provide the seed or create the harvest—those are God's responsibilities. We must do the work, but the "blessing pipeline" all belongs to God.

Here is the most amazing part: we get to partner with him and be
part of the process. Our "giving valve" must be open and ready to receive
what he has for us, so that we can pass it on to others.

10. Our giving honors God.

*For the ministry of this service is not only supplying the needs of
the saints but is also overflowing in many thanksgivings to God. By
their approval of this service, they will glorify God because of your
submission that comes from your confession of the gospel of Christ,
and the generosity of your contribution for them and for all others,
while they long for you and pray for you, because of the surpassing
grace of God upon you. Thanks be to God for his inexpressible gift!*
(2 Cor. 9:12–15)

Paul concludes this extraordinary passage of Scripture by reminding us
that giving is ultimately an act of worship. God supplies the seed, he
brings the harvest, and the end result is that we bring honor to him since
we get to participate in serving others.

Serving is not a burden—it is a privilege and honor. No matter
whether you're an entrepreneur, a worker in a factor, or the president of
a billion-dollar company, you are always serving someone. If you are a
person of faith, you are ultimately serving God.

In the movie *Gladiator*, Russell Crowe plays Maximus, a general in the Roman army. The opening scene shows Maximus preparing his troops for battle again the Germanic tribes. Just before the battle commences, Maximus delivers a rousing speech to the troops, reminding them, "What we do in life echoes in eternity."

This truth that applies to our giving as well. If we can put on the correct lenses and see our giving from God's point of view, this new perspective will help us see that our giving does indeed echo in eternity.

Keys to Performance-Driven Giving

In order to develop a deeper spiritual perspective on giving, consider the following:

1. What is your vision for giving in your life? What would your life look like in five or ten years if you became a bigger giver? Take a few moments to write out a vision statement for giving in your life.

2. Look over the two misunderstandings about money we listed earlier in the chapter. Do you agree with our perspective? Have you ever thought about money as "God-given energy"?

3. Review the list of ten principles on giving from 2 Corinthians 8–9. Choose two of them and brainstorm how you can put them into practice within the next seven days.

The Giving Equation

There are two mindsets when it comes to giving: a scarcity mindset, and an abundance mindset. We'll look at these in more detail later on, but let's briefly explore them here in the context of how money works in God's way of doing things.

As kids, we all learned addition, subtraction, multiplication, and division. These mathematical functions apply not only to numbers, but also to money. Obviously, we don't want to focus on scarcity, so division and subtraction have no place within God's view of money. Our goal is more abundance and blessing.

That's why we must focus on addition and multiplication. When you decide to work with God in your finances and giving, He can do incredible things, more than you ever thought possible! And when you factor in the element of time, the possibilities become endless.

Here is the Giving Equation shown in mathematical terms:

$$(You + God) \times Time = Unlimited\ Impact$$

If you have been shying away from God's involvement in your finances, this is a great opportunity to reconsider your position. Giving doesn't *subtract* from your life—it *adds* joy, blessings, relationships, impact, success, and so much more.

It is critical that we do not *divide* our lives into areas where we let God in and areas where we keep Him out. We are integrated beings, and God wants to bless every area of our lives, including our finances. He takes our meager abilities and resources and *multiplies* their impact over time.

A Conversation with Ray Edwards, Communications Strategist and Copywriter

We realize this chapter presents a lot of concepts that may be new to you. It's a challenging prospect to embrace a whole new view of giving...or what you might call a "God's-eye view." In order to help us flesh out these concepts, we are thrilled to present an interview with our good friend Ray Edwards.

Ray is a communications strategist and copywriter, and the author of *Permission to Prosper: How to Be Rich beyond Your Wildest Dreams*. His podcast, the Ray Edwards Show, is consistently one of the top-rated shows in Apple Podcasts and has been downloaded over 1.5 million times.

Ray has worked on copy and marketing with some of the most powerful voices in leadership and business, helping generate an estimated $400 million in revenue for clients such as Tony Robbins, Michael Hyatt, Dan Miller, Jeff Goins, Jack Canfield, Frank Kern, and many more.

We began our conversation by Ray to help us understand the concept of "prosperity."

> *I believe in a biblical context. Prosperity is living the fullest expression of what God has in store for us. And that can be summed up in the way it was summed up in the New Testament: The kingdom of God is not about eating and drinking and all the stuff that we have. It's about righteousness, peace, and joy in the Holy Spirit.*
>
> *If the kingdom, the King's domain, is within us, then we should feel a sense of righteousness, peace, and joy. And that comes from a feeling of abundance.*
>
> *There's a great line in the twenty-third Psalm. It says, "The Lord is my shepherd. I shall not want." Another translation says it this way: "The Lord is my shepherd. I lack nothing."*
>
> *This is what Jesus was talking about in Matthew 6:33 when he said, "Seek first the kingdom of God and his righteousness, and all these things shall be added unto you."*
>
> *We're seeking the kingdom of God, which is the domain of the King. That's what "King" means. If we look within and we seek first his kingdom and his righteousness, not our own righteousness, we won't need to be concerned with what to eat or drink, what the market is doing, where I'm going to live, and so many other things. We don't need to worry. That is true prosperity.*

This is a difficult concept for many people in the faith community because we often associate righteousness with poverty. We asked Ray why this belief is completely mistaken.

Let's be clear: Material things make us neither rich nor prosperous in any permanent, lasting sense. We came into this world naked with nothing. That's exactly how we're going to go out. Life has a one hundred percent mortality rate.

Everything we have between now and then is profit, wealth, and prosperity, but those things do not make us prosperous. The prosperity we have comes from within. We are what God says we are.

You are enormously wealthy and prosperous because you're a son or a daughter of the King. He owns everything. It's all just on loan to us. We're temporary stewards. And yet, because of our kinship with the King, his prosperity is our prosperity. Regardless of what our bank balance is, we are incredibly rich.

If we are incredibly rich, it means we can give freely because God's riches never run out. However, many people who are in desperate straits financially may have a hard time feeling they can give. Ray gave several great tips for giving when you don't have a lot of money.

Here's something you can give with no money in your pocket. You can give your attention to the person right in front of you. You can give your presence to the people you're with. You can be there in that moment.

Today's world is so interesting because people are continually projecting themselves to somewhere other than where they are. If they're waiting in a line somewhere for the bank teller, or a restaurant, or at a coffee shop, they're looking at their phones. They're thinking about their to-do list. They're thinking about an upcoming meeting. They're not truly present doing what they're doing while they are doing it.

You can give someone a smile. You can be kind to the person behind the cash register. It may not seem like a big deal to you, but it may make all the difference to them in the world. If you have no money and you have children and a family at home, you can give them your time and your attention as you play with them.

Listen to them. Talk about their day. Kids know the secret of contentment.

They are happy to go to Disney World. They're also happy to build a castle out of cardboard boxes in the backyard and have an entire adventure in an afternoon. We could learn a lot from children, which I think is why it's stolen. You need to become like one of these little children to enter into the kingdom.

In our final question to Ray, we asked him to share some ways that business leaders and entrepreneurs can practice generosity.

Generosity can mean giving money to charities, your church, or missionaries. That's a great thing to do, but there are other ways to be generous as well.

Another way to be generous is to give enormous value in your marketing and your advertising. You can deliver information and helpful education. I'm a big believer in something called education-based marketing, which means that even in your marketing, you're helping people achieve a better quality of life.

You can make the very best products and overdeliver on quality. Business in and of itself creates more prosperity. It creates prosperity for your employees; for your vendors; for your suppliers; for the service providers who provide cable, electricity, power, and water for your office buildings; for the people who transport your goods; and for the people who receive them. Something you did made their life better, more financially feasible, or more profitable. Good, honest business in and of itself is an act of generosity.

And then you can do simple things, like pay your team better than they expect. Pay them better than average for your industry. Be generous in their pay. Be generous in your pricing. Be generous in the amount of time and attention you give to your community. Generosity is not a separate activity that we practice and tick it off a list. It's a way of life.

Thanks, Ray! We are grateful for your much-needed perspective on giving and generosity.

Ray's website is https://rayedwards.com. We encourage you to check out his book, *Permission to Prosper*, which is a fantastic guide to help you become more prosperous in all the ways that matter. To listen to the entire interview, go to PerformanceDrivenThinking.com/Giving or scan the QR code to visit the page.

We also recommend connecting with Ray on social media:

Facebook: https://www.facebook.com/RayEdwardsOnline
LinkedIn: https://www.linkedin.com/in/rayedwardsinternational
Twitter: https://twitter.com/rayedwards
Instagram: https://www.instagram.com/rayedwards
YouTube: https://www.youtube.com/user/RayEdwardsTV
Podcast: https://rayedwards.com/podcast-archives

CHAPTER 3

Mindset: The Root of Performance-Driven Giving

Make all you can, save all you can, give all you can.
—John Wesley

Have you ever broken a bone? If so, you know it's a painful process that can involve many weeks of healing. After you break a bone, the doctor will set it before putting on a cast. Setting the bone ensures that it is aligned the right way and will grow properly.

When it is done correctly, the bone can grow back even stronger than before. When it is not done correctly, the bone will be out of alignment and will cause significant problems as time goes by.

Just as a bone can be set, so can your mind. A mindset is literally how you "set" (orient) your mind. This is the root of performance-driven giving, because your thinking determines everything else in your life. Remember, performance-driving thinking is "the thought process that connects the *desire* to perform with the *will* to perform a specific task or goal." If you want to change your outcome, it begins with your mindset.

As Earl Nightingale famously said, "You become what you think about." Now that we have established how giving helps you become great, as well as the spiritual foundation of giving, we will explore another foundational aspect of giving: your mindset. This is a critical component of giving because your outlook on life determines how you approach everything else.

In her landmark book *Mindset: The New Psychology of Success*, Carol Dweck wrote that there are two kinds of mindsets: a fixed mindset and a growth mindset. A fixed mindset continues to operate the way it has always operated. It is not capable of change or development.

A fixed mindset will continue to shrink because the world is always changing and developing. A person with a fixed mindset will become more irrelevant and out of touch over time.

However, a person with a growth mindset will keep changing as time goes by because they will always be assimilating new information. They will adapt to changing situations and seize new opportunities to put what they have learned into practice. We want you to develop a growth mindset because a growing mind is a giving mind.

But how do we do that? What are some practical ways to grow your mindset so you can increase your giving in multiple ways? There are many ways to do this, but we recommend focusing on the three R's of growing your mindset: reading, relationships, and remembering.

Read: Expand Your Mind with Great Books

Charlie "Tremendous" Jones was famous for saying, "You will be the same person in five years as you are today except for the people you meet and the books you read." He knew that reading could have a powerful impact on your life, as well as those you influence.

But why? What is the unique power of books to change your life?

A book represents the research, wisdom, or knowledge that an author has taken years to acquire. Yet you can consume a book in just a few hours. Every time you read a great book, it is the equivalent of downloading part of an author's brain. If you wanted to have a conversation with some of the world's great thinkers and leaders, you would probably have a hard time getting a meeting with them. But through the power of books, you can have immediate access to anyone in history who has taken the time to record their knowledge. Sometimes, a book represents a whole lifetime of wisdom.

Even if you only read a couple of books a month, in a year's time you can accumulate hundreds of years' worth of wisdom, learning, and insights. So much of the time, we settle for binge-watching television shows or spending our time in other nonproductive ways. But reading can expand your thinking and introduce you to ideas you would otherwise not have.

As the founder of Morgan James Publishing, I (David) believe in the power of books! Our authors and our team members work hard to write and publish books that will literally change the world.

Since you're reading this book, we assume you already believe in the power of books. In fact, you may have experienced a common problem with people who want to grow in their personal and professional lives: They have too many books they want to read.

We recommend reading from the following seven categories. Each category of books can help you become a better giver.

1. Fiction

Many leaders and business professionals believe fiction is a waste of time, but we disagree, because stories are one of the best teaching tools. In fact, Jesus himself used stories (parables) as his primary way of getting his message across. Reading great fiction, especially the classics, can help you get a better grasp on human nature.

Fiction also gives you a great point of dialogue with the culture, which is an important approach if we are to be able to speak with others who share a different faith perspective.

2. Biography

A great biography can help you understand the experiences, triumphs, and failures of another person. In a world that is increasingly polarized and divided, we can all use a little more empathy and understanding.

When you gain a perspective through another person's life story, you often come to understand your own life better. You can see the world through their lens, and your own lens becomes clearer.

A sense of giving requires that we value other people and believe they are worthy. Experiencing other people's stories is a great step toward that.

3. Personal Growth

This type of book can consist of many different categories, but they are all concerned with one thing: giving you the tools and resources to improve some aspect of your life. While fiction and biographies can help you gain a better perspective, nonfiction books are written to solve problems.

We encourage you to read personal growth books regularly because they will expand your leadership and help you become stronger, healthier, and more productive. In turn, this helps you increase your capacity to give more.

4. Finance

You can have the right heart and motives, and even some great strategies, but if you don't have financial resources, you will be limited in your options, and limited in your ability to help others financially.

Of course, there are many ways to give, and money is just one of them. However, it's vital to get your own financial house in order so you can feel less stress around money and be able to bless others. We recommend books that will help you save, invest, budget, and give you a better understanding of how money works.

5. Spiritual Development

As we talked about in chapter 2, there is an important spiritual component to giving. Giving is only one aspect of a fully developed spiritual life. Books on spiritual development can help develop this part of your life, which is often ignored by those who want greater success at work.

It's easy to put the focus on status or material possessions. While those can be important, we are eternal beings who must not neglect that component of our lives. And of course, we recommend reading the Bible regularly as part of your overall spiritual growth.

6. Relationships

Highly driven people sometimes focus on giving in ways they can measure with numbers, accomplishments, or titles. It can be harder to pay attention to relationships because it's not possible to measure them.

But relationships are one of the most important ways that we give, as we will see in later chapters. Read books on love, marriage, parenting, conflict management, psychology, and other elements of healthy relationships so you don't miss this component of an important way that we give.

7. Business and Entrepreneurship

Many people will remain in a traditional job their whole lives, and there is nothing wrong with that. But we encourage you to consider how you might add value to the world and increase your income by starting a business.

It's easy to feel intimidated by this, especially when you don't have any experience. However, today you can learn just about anything with the help of mentors, online resources, courses, or books. When you understand the greater economic engine, as well as how to make money by creating value, your potential to help others financially will skyrocket.

Relationships: Strengthen Your Ties with Givers

No one develops a better mindset in a vacuum. If we are to grow to our full potential, it requires relationships with other people. Remember the quote from Charlie Jones earlier in the chapter? A vital component of success is our relationship with others. Therefore, we must seek out opportunities to grow these relationships and strengthen our ties with people who are givers.

When we think of "networking," a picture comes to mind of a smarmy business gathering where everyone is looking out for themselves. What we are talking about is the opposite of that! Good networking and effective relationships are all about mutually serving and adding value. If you don't have those as a fundamental way of living, no amount of strategic networking will pay off.

Here are three excellent ways to build relationships with givers.

1. Engage with givers on social media.

As soon as we say this, red flags will go up for some people. Why? Because social media is well known as a place where a lot of conflict and bad behavior happens. While that is true, social media can also be a place where friendships and lasting connections are made.

You can engage with positive and generous people on social media by commenting on posts, answering questions in groups, and participating in discussions. Many people make social media success too complicated. It's just like real life—you build good relationships by being a giver first. You show up and add value as well as encourage others.

It's fairly simple, but when you do this consistently, you can connect with an astounding number of leaders who will encourage you as a giver.

2. Start or join a mastermind group.

Mastermind groups can take many forms. However, the general idea is that you meet with a small group (usually twelve people or less) to encourage each other in your success. You brainstorm, troubleshoot problems, and lift each other up to a higher level. Masterminds operate on the principle of synergy: When people come together for a common purpose, the outcome is greater than the individual effort.

A major factor in the success of a mastermind group is the members themselves. They have to be positive and wanting to grow and learn. They need to want to help other people succeed. They can't be in it just for themselves.

You can start a mastermind group or join an existing one. It all depends on your goals and what you want to get out of it. Regardless of the structure, you will have a great experience if the group members are positive thinkers who are there to serve. The mastermind will almost certainly add value to your life, and you will be able to add much value to others as well.

3. Interview other givers.

Interviews are a powerful medium where you can ask questions and share the guest's wisdom with your audience. The two most popular formats are blog posts and podcasts. If you have a podcast or have considered starting one, we recommend that format because you can hear the interview audio rather than reading a transcription or summary.

Podcasting is powerful medium because it gives you a space to invite leaders and influencers for a conversation. This is a great way to build relationships because often times, the best conversations happen off the mic, before or after the actual interview.

If you decide to do a podcast, be aware that it takes time to plan, record, edit, and publish a podcast. Make sure to ask good questions and create clean audio that sounds as professional as possible. Then share it with as many people as you can. We recommend checking out the *Morgan James Radio* podcast as an example of a show that features great interviews with leaders and givers.

The main idea here is to seek out spaces where givers are located. This can include social media groups, masterminds, and podcasts, as well as many other methods we could mention. Remember that the medium is not as important as simply seeking out givers and building relationships in a natural way.

Remember: Show Gratitude to Others

Gratitude is one of the most powerful drivers of giving. When we purposefully think about how others have positively impacted our lives, gratitude is easy! But we sometimes forgot to express it. Here are a few ways to show gratitude and remember how others have blessed us.

Share and review other people's content.

As children, we learned that "sharing is caring." But as we get older, sometimes we forgot to share things that impact us. It might be a book, blog post, article, podcast, or a sermon. If it has impacted you, it will probably help other people as well. A powerful way to exponentially increase the power of good content is to share it on social media, via email, or even by word of mouth.

Here's a simple example. Let's say a friend of yours wrote a great blog post. All it takes is a few seconds to share it on social media. That way, many others can benefit from it. Plus, your author friend will appreciate your thoughtfulness. Everybody wins! You can do the same thing for any type of content. Many times we think that promoting other people somehow diminishes us, but that's not true. Promoting others actually increases your credibility because we are being helpful and generous.

Content creators also appreciate ratings and reviews for their books and music. It just takes a few moments to leave a review, but it means the world to the person who created it. Your small act of generosity helps create goodwill and keeps the cycle of giving going strong.

Send gifts and handwritten cards.

Handwritten thank-you cards are a rarity in today's world, which is filled with digital communication. The reason? They're inconvenient to create. Yet that is precisely the reason why we should send handwritten cards—because the receiver knows we put some effort into it.

The same could be said for sending gifts. There is a whole industry devoted to the art and science of giving gifts, but the main idea is to send a gift that is meaningful to the recipient.

Say thank you.

This might be the most underrated yet simple practice of all. How many times do you say thank you during a regular day? Have you ever counted? The result may not be as many times as you think!

We challenge you to be more intentional with showing gratitude to the people in your everyday life by sharing a simple thank you. Just being more mindful of this tiny act will help make you more aware of how gratitude impacts you and others.

Are You a Reservoir or River?

As we conclude this chapter on mindset, we want to present a metaphor that can be helpful for honestly evaluating your level of giving and prompting you to a life of greater generosity.

There are two kinds of people in this world: reservoirs and rivers. A reservoir is a point of collection for water, whether that water comes from a stream or river, rain, or another source. It receives, but does not give.

Many people are like reservoirs. They collect everything they can and hang on to it because they are afraid of losing it. They have a scarcity mindset that prevents them from sharing and giving. They see everyone as a competitor in the game of life.

A river, on the other hand, is a channel for water that is constantly flowing. You can never step into the same river twice because it is always changing. The riverbed changes over time because it is shaped by the water. The whole function of a river is to carry water from one place to another.

Givers are like rivers. They have an abundance mindset that allows them to not only receive blessings but give them away as well. They know that whatever they give, it will come back to them in surprising ways. Givers are not materialistic because they realize they can never truly own anything since it all belongs to God.

In our modern world, we all face the challenge of materialism. We are surrounded by shiny objects. We are bombarded with hundreds of marketing messages every day that tell us life is only worth living if you have the most toys.

Givers know better. They understand that the good life is one where you have abundance, but it's not only in material things. They have an abundance mindset that helps them see the big picture. We hope this chapter has challenged you to grow your mindset by intentionally reading great books, growing your relationships with givers, and remembering what others have done for you.

Keys to Performance-Driven Giving

In order to develop a mindset of giving, consider the following:

1. Review the types of books we mentioned earlier in the chapter. What are the most recent books you have read in each category? Choose one or two books from each of those categories to read in the next year. If you need ideas, ask a few friends for the titles of recent good books they have read.

2. Don't be overwhelmed by all the ways you can develop relationships with givers. Choose one of the strategies we mentioned earlier in the chapter and give it a try this week.

3. How is your gratitude practice? If you don't currently send handwritten thank-you notes, make it a goal to send one per day this

week. You will be surprised at how meaningful this is to the person who receives it.

How to Read More in Less Time

As we have noted in this chapter, reading is a key element in your growth as a giver. But when you look at the stack of books on your shelf that you haven't read, do you feel stressed because you don't have enough time to read? Here are a few ways to get more reading done in less time.

Have a set time each day to read.

There is great power in establishing a routine. No matter what time of day is best for you, pick a time and stick with it. Maybe it's early morning before you start your workday. Maybe it's during lunch. Maybe it's in the evening or during bedtime. Whatever time you choose, set an appointment with yourself and keep it.

You can also attach reading to another activity. Knowing as habit stacking, this is a powerful way to make a habit easier. For example, you can stack reading on top of flossing or brushing your teeth. The original activity becomes a trigger for the habit you want to develop.

Keep a book where you will see it every day.

You might keep a book on your nightstand, on your desk, or even in your car if you read while waiting to pick your kid up from school. When you see the book, it's a trigger to start reading. If you prefer ebooks or audiobooks, set a reminder on your calendar to read since you don't use a print copy.

Set a reading goal.

For example, you might set a goal such as reading ten pages per day, one book every two weeks, or ten books per quarter. The important

---

thing is to set a goal that is manageable within your current season of life and responsibilities.

Read with a partner.

When you involve other people in a goal or a habit, it's a powerful motivator to follow through on your commitment. Why? Because you don't want to be the one who doesn't come through. There are lots of reading groups, masterminds, and study groups that go through a book together.

You can also go through a book with a friend. The important thing is having someone to discuss the reading with. In Western culture, we have made reading a mostly solitary activity. Our individualism often robs us of the opportunity to process our learning with others. Everybody comes out stronger when we learn together.

Listen to audiobooks.

The average work commute in the United States is twenty-five minutes each way. You can use that time for listening to music and the latest news on talk radio, or you can use it to learn. Zig Ziglar called this "automobile university." You can listen to several audiobooks per month this way.

Read books that interest you, and stop reading ones that don't.

As readers, we have a built-in guilt that we must finish a book. But if you've read part of a book and you're not getting anything out of it, set it aside and read something else. It doesn't mean the book is bad. It just means that it's not the right book for you at this time.

There are more books published every week than you could possibly read in a lifetime, and life is too short to spend it doing things that don't interest you.

Always have a book with you.

You would be surprised at all the little spare moments we have throughout the day. Perhaps it's waiting to pick up your kid from school, waiting for a meeting to start, waiting at the DMV, waiting for your spouse while they are in a store, and a hundred other little moments. If you have a book with you, use those few minutes for reading.

Let's say you have three of those times each day when you're just waiting for something, and each of those times is five minutes. That's fifteen minutes a day, or an hour and fifteen minutes for the whole work week. In a month's time, you can read two good-sized books, just by taking a book with you wherever you go, and using those spare little moments during the day.

Use some of your entertainment time for reading.

This is one of the most obvious ways to get more reading done. If you spend a lot of time watching television or other entertainment, allocate some of that time to reading. If you use only fifteen minutes of your entertainment time per day for reading, you can read a couple of books per month without taking any extra time out of your schedule.

A Conversation with Tommy Breedlove, Founder of the Legendary Life Movement

You've spent a chapter learning about three important R's—reading, relationships, and remembering (gratitude). These are key factors in developing the mindset of a giver. We wanted to close out this chapter by interviewing a leader known for helping others master their mindset of generosity and success. Ladies and gentlemen, we are happy to introduce Tommy Breedlove!

Tommy is the author of the *Wall Street Journal* and *USA Today* bestselling book *Legendary: A Simple Playbook for Building and Living a Leg-*

endary Life and Being Remembered as a Legend. His purpose in life is to guide ambitious people to become more successful and confident spouses, parents, and leaders in their businesses and communities. Tommy is not only a success, relationship, and mindset coach, but he is also a regular featured keynote speaker at global events.

Tommy started his twenty-year corporate career at one of the largest financial consulting firms in the world and eventually became a share-holder, the International Practice Leader, and a member of the board of directors for one of the largest public accounting and financial firms in the southeast United States. At the top of his career, Tommy experienced a transformational moment that inspired him to walk away from the corporate world and follow his true calling of rescuing ambitious people from themselves, just like he did for himself.

Tommy now serves clients and audiences everywhere by empowering them to build and live Legendary Lives. We began our conversation on one theme of living the good life. We explored what this means and how giving plays a part in the good life.

> *For me, everything, including living the good life, starts and ends with giving, especially giving to ourselves—this is also tied to our purpose.*
>
> *In order to truly serve and love others, we must serve ourselves first. Therefore, living the good life is about rest, continuous learning and growing, being open-minded, and traveling, as well as building our spiritual, mental, emotional, and physical muscles each and every day. We must stop putting ourselves last as being a martyr does not benefit anyone.*
>
> *However, we can't live the good life without understanding and working in our purpose. I believe every human being on earth, until their very last breath, has a purpose. I also believe our purpose changes depending on the seasons of our lives. As our desires and circumstances change, our purpose changes. Serving others via our purpose and living the good life are very much in sync to me.*

Purpose is being part of something bigger than ourselves. It's about helping our fellow human beings and leaving our beautiful planet a little bit better than we found it. We can travel, eat the greatest foods, have the shiny things, and experience all life has to offer, but without intention or purpose, we lack fulfillment, happiness, and significance in our lives.

Our purpose gives us true fulfillment and connects us with God. I know a lot of people in my network who are very financially successful and surround themselves with all that money can buy. Time and time again they come to me because they're not fulfilled and happy. Why? Because they lack purpose and meaning to their lives. Money is super important, especially when it comes to experiencing life to its fullest and creating great impact, but money without purpose or a solid foundation of goodness and serving is a curse and not a blessing.

When we live with purpose, we are living for something bigger than ourselves and living a life with no regrets. At the end of the day, I want all of us to say, "I served. I laughed. I loved. I cared." That's living the good life! Does it really get any better than that?

Well said, Tommy! We couldn't agree more. And what if someone does not already have a generous mindset that is driven by purpose?

The first thing they must understand is they are not alone. It is A-OK if someone has not yet discovered their purpose or wants to change their mindset from fear to abundance. They just have to want to serve or give back to their community in some way. We must remember that our mindset and most of our fears and limiting beliefs were taught to us by our parents, TV, our teachers, and the culture that surrounds us. All the beliefs that were taught to us, that no longer serve us, most of which are probably untrue, can always be rewired.

We can choose to live within our value systems with a mindset of purpose, courage, confidence, and gratitude. We can choose to see the good in the world and not focus on the bad. To sum up life, the only power we truly have is the power to choose our thoughts, actions, and attitudes towards ourselves and others.

If we don't have a mindset of giving, we are living with a scarcity mindset. This way of thinking is focused on the self and ego. At the end of the day, a life of scarcity, fear, and unhealthy competition will not reward us as much as a life of abundance, loving, serving, and with a giving mindset.

We can rewire our hearts and minds from scarcity to abundance. This is a practice, much like going to the gym to build our physical muscles. We must put the same intention and action toward our spirit, heart, and mind muscles in order to gain self-confidence, self-love, and self-respect.

There are many simple tools to do this, which I talk about extensively in my book, Legendary. *First, we have to eliminate the negative influences in our lives. We must distance ourselves from negative people who are takers, judgmental, angry, eat up in fear, or unhappy. Light attracts light, and darkness attracts darkness. If you're not hanging around with successful, loving, giving, charitable people, you're not going to be one, and vice versa.*

Regular practices of gratitude, affirmations, meditation, and forgiveness, along with reading positive books on self-development, also help us grow stronger and more confident.

That leads perfectly into the next question. Many people love to give but have trouble receiving because they don't have a lot of self-confidence or self-esteem. How can someone stay open to the gifts others have for them?

That's very true, many people feel they can't receive love because they're not worthy. They feel they're not skinny enough, smart enough, rich enough, etc. Social media has taken this cultural dilemma and put it on steroids with everyone displaying themselves as "Facebook and Instagram fabulous."

The most important thing for all of us to remember is that we are not alone. We all have our own fears and insecurities. Not one single person on earth does not have things they regret and/or worry about. Also, issues of depression, suicide, domestic violence, and alcohol and drug abuse are off the charts in modern times. We must talk about these issues and recognize that there is hope if we simply lean into vulnerability and authentic conversations and do the deep inner work.

A great way to combat the "We're not good enough" insecurities and fears is by practicing gratitude, meditation, daily reading, and prayer as well as surrounding ourselves with positivity and feeding our soul with goodness. Remember: garbage into our minds and souls (social media, twenty-four-hour news, reality TV, etc.) equals garbage out (negative thinking). Goodness and love in equals goodness and love out. Let's continue moving forward and investing in ourselves. Over time, we will see the good in the world and begin to know that we are enough, loveable, valuable, and worthy. All of us!

Thank you, Tommy! Those are words everyone needs to hear.

Tommy's website is https://tommybreedlove.com. We also hope you will check out his book, *Legendary*, which will help you build a variety of key practices into your life to begin living a life with purpose, meaning, and significance. To listen to the entire interview, go to PerformanceDrivenThinking.com/Giving or scan the QR code to visit the page.

We also recommend following Tommy on social media:

Facebook: https://www.facebook.com/tommybreedlovelegendary
LinkedIn: https://www.linkedin.com/company/tommy-breedlove
Instagram: https://www.instagram.com/tommybreedlove

CHAPTER 4

Indifference: The Biggest Obstacle to Giving

If you will live like no one else, later you can live like no one else.
—Dave Ramsey

In the classic children's book *Pierre*, written by Maurice Sendak, we meet a young boy who doesn't care about anything. No matter what his mother or father says, no matter how they try to motivate him, he always responds with "I don't care!"

When a hungry lion pays a call and ultimately eats Pierre, it is only then that he starts to care. (Fortunately, the doctor was able to retrieve Pierre from the lion.) The story ends with these words: "The moral of Pierre is: CARE!"

Pierre may be a book for children, but it contains a lot of wisdom for adults. Many people in our culture today are indifferent to the needs of others and the opportunities they have to give. The *Merriam-Webster.com Dictionary* defines "indifferent" this way: "marked by a lack of interest, enthusiasm, or concern for something."

There are many obstacles that prevent people from giving. Most people believe the enemy of giving is "taking." But the biggest enemy is indifference. In this chapter, we will look at the reasons for it, how to handle it, as well as the symptoms of indifference.

The Roots of Indifference

Before we look at solutions for helping people overcome their indifference, we must first understand the reasons for it. There are several important roots that cause our indifference.

Distractions

In recent years, movie theaters have undergone many different kinds of transformations. They have upgraded projection systems, installed new sound systems, and offered new kinds of dining experiences. And oddly enough, they have cracked down on people using their cell phones.

You would be hard-pressed to go to a theater today and not see someone using their cell phone during the movie. This is a big problem because it distracts both the moviegoer and everyone around them from the main event.

This is a perfect metaphor for the world today: We are distracted and missing the big picture of life. On any given day, we spend two to three hours on social media, in addition to work, family, church, hobbies, and social obligations. How do we fit it all in? The truth is that we often don't. We are like squirrels who are constantly distracted, moving from one thing to the next. The result is that we don't have the mental capacity to notice the needs of others around us.

This not only applies to our productivity. It also applies to our giving. Whenever we are trying to juggle too many things in life, not to mention all of our distractions from social media, it is nearly impossible to think about anything but ourselves.

Denial

When we do see genuine needs, it is not difficult to deny them. It is easy to believe that the wealthy, the government, social programs, or churches will take care of the needs of other people.

We continue to be influenced by media outlets, which are focused on the urgent. They are most interested in stories and information that creates hype and results in the most clicks or views. The most important needs in the world don't always make for the most exciting stories.

We are also in denial about other people's needs because we simply don't realize they exist. Most of us live a life that is carefully curated to produce the most favorable image. We select the right photographs and social media posts to show to the world. It is hard to admit our real needs because we don't want to look weak. Therefore others may not know what our needs are, and we may not know other people's real needs.

Doubt

When people give to causes or charities, it is easy to doubt whether their gift is making any difference. There are two reasons for this.

First, it is sometimes hard to tell how your giving directly impacts lives. Most organizations create charts and reports detailing all kinds of data about their giving. But at the end of the day, people don't care about data—they care about the humans that the data represents. It's hard to feel engaged in giving unless you know the stories of at least some of the people your giving impacts.

The second reason that people are sometimes in doubt about giving is because they can mistrust the organizations themselves. In the last few years we've heard many stories of corporate greed and abuse of power. Of course, this is nothing new. As long as there have been people in power, there has been bad behavior. As long as we are fallen, broken human beings, leaders will fall short.

However, the bad behavior of a few high-profile individuals hurts everyone. Trust in the government and other organizations is at an all-time low. It can be hard to convince donors that they are making a difference if the donors don't trust them in the first place.

Despair

News outlets have reported recently that suicide rates are on the rise. With the current climate of world upheaval and an unpredictable economy, no one would be surprised to see this increase even further. We are in the middle of a mental health crisis. Many people have simply given up hope.

Anyone who has experienced depression or other mental illness knows how debilitating it can be. If you have a loved one who has suffered from mental illness, that can be equally as draining. Despair, hopelessness, and depression not only send the person down a dark path within themselves, but they also prevent them from bringing their true value to the world. You cannot give what you do not have.

It has been said that "hurt people, hurt people." It is also true that hurt people ignore others because they do not have the emotional capacity to pay attention to other people's needs. Although mental illness is rarely mentioned in connection with giving and generosity, it deeply affects a person's ability to fully show up in every area of their life.

Debt

The average American has four credit cards and nearly $40,000 of debt, excluding their home mortgage. This is a major factor that impacts people's ability to help others, but not just from a financial standpoint. When people are in debt, they are stressed and consumed with fear. This can lead to despair and, in the worst cases, people losing so much hope that they consider taking their own lives.

There are many reasons for a family's debt, but generally we can attribute it to two reasons: consumerism and a lack of discipline. When they are brought together, it is a deadly combination. We desire all the objects that other people, but if we lack the discipline to save, invest, and give, it's a deadly cycle.

This is a picture of the typical American family: Both parents go to jobs where they feel underpaid and undervalued. They are stressed about money and worried about paying their bills. They don't have much in savings. To deal with the stress, they buy more things and distract themselves with their media and entertainment. They don't face their financial problems head-on, which leads to more stress, more debt, and often to despair, since they don't believe they will ever get out of their hole.

This paints a pretty gloomy picture of the average American family—one where most people are simply indifferent to giving. Perhaps it describes *your* family. If so, don't be discouraged. We have some suggestions not just for your family, but for anyone who wants to help others give more.

Keys to Handling Indifference

Indifference takes on many different forms, and therefore you can deal with it a variety of different ways. However, these suggestions can help almost any situation when taken together.

Connect with the humans on the other side of giving.

Although our giving does not take place in a vacuum, sometimes it can feel that way. When we are giving to organizations, we often don't see the result of our volunteer efforts or the financial help that we offer. When possible, try to discover the human beings who benefit from your giving.

One example is World Vision, an organization that provides relief to children around the world. They do a fantastic job of helping their donors make a personal connection with the children they support. The donors and recipients can send letters back and forth, and they have also sent cards featuring a short video of supported child. This has a powerful effect of seeing the difference you have made in a real person's life.

You can also get personally involved with recipients by serving in a homeless shelter, food bank, or soup kitchen. These are wonderful opportunities to connect face-to-face with people whom you are serving. It is easy to see people as a faceless sea of humanity, but each one of these people has a story and a name.

If time and resources permit, you can also take a mission trip or serve abroad. Not everyone has the opportunity to do this, but a mission trip can be a powerful and life-changing experience that can give you a broader perspective on other people's needs.

Limit your distractions.

Technology is a force that can take over our whole lives if we allow it. This is what the creators of our gadgets and social media intend! The more time we spend on our devices and entertainment, the more they profit.

Limiting your distractions starts with being intentional. It doesn't mean you get rid of all your devices or you never watch movies or TV shows. But it does mean that with a little effort, you can free up a lot of mental space.

A great place to start is by turning off devices past a certain time of night, for example 9 p.m. The blue light from your device is not only interrupting your sleep pattern, but the notifications and distractions on those devices wreak havoc with your ability to rest and relax. If your brain is always engaged in your technology, it never has a chance to do a deeper reflection and to develop creative ideas.

We also suggest shutting off unnecessary notifications when you are doing important work. You can put your phone on airplane mode or and shut off other alerts such as email and apps. If need be, work in a different place so you do not have to deal with as many interruptions and distractions.

Sometimes it is very simple things that can help us get free from distractions and have a healthier life so we can breathe emotionally and mentally.

Stay emotionally healthy.

When we talk about mental health, we don't just necessarily mean those who suffer from clinical depression. Mental health is important for everyone, even if you don't consider yourself depressed or have not been diagnosed with a mental illness.

Let's start with the basics. Are you taking care of yourself? Do you take one day off per week at least? Do you do things that are relaxing? Are you getting enough sleep? Are you eating healthy and exercising? Those are all important aspects of being emotionally healthy.

It's also vital to maintain a group of close friends. A big part of mental health is knowing that you are part of a community of people who care for you. If you're not, reach out to someone in your circle and invite them to lunch or get on a call with them. You would be surprised at the number of other people in your life who are feeling isolated and lonely as well. You might just be the solution to your own problem.

Of course, if you are suffering symptoms of depression or going through a personal crisis, consult a doctor who can prescribe the correct pathway forward for you to deal with any serious issues in your life. We want you to be healthy, whole, and energized so you can show up and give your best self to the world.

Pay attention to the needs around you.

When we use the phrase "pay attention," we do so very intentionally. Paying attention literally means that it's going to cost you something. The attention you give to others must be taken away from something else, and that's a good thing. We have to intentionally choose to break out of a distracted mode and begin to really see the needs of those around us.

It doesn't mean you necessarily have to go to a foreign country to do this. In fact, you can do it right now wherever you are. Who is around you? Your family, team members at work? Those on social media or others you have contacted today? Do you know what they need? Do you know what's going on in their lives?

Giving is not always a big flashy affair. In fact, sometimes the most meaningful giving is what we give of ourselves. It could mean listening to your child or spouse who's had a bad day, and being empathetic with them. It could be listening to a colleague's suggestion at work. But it could also mean giving to a homeless person or responding to a call for volunteers at church.

It doesn't take much to become aware of the needs around us. It just means that we are intentional and that we choose to not be sucked into all the distractions around us.

Reduce your debt.

This is a far more complicated topic then we can address in detail here. But the main point is this: Most people know what they need to do to get out of debt, but it is difficult to do it because it is an emotional issue. For example, everyone knows that they need to save money, invest, make more money, and get rid of debt to have a better financial footing. But if it were easy, nobody would have debt.

A great first step to dealing with debt is to track your finances and make a budget. You can use a simple spreadsheet, an app, or a computer program. The tool does not matter as much as the regular discipline of seeing where your money actually goes. As Dave Ramsey says, make sure every dollar has a job. This means planning in advance how much you're going to spend on various categories for the coming month.

It is also helpful to have a conversation with your spouse about money and how you can begin getting out of debt. If you are single, enlist the help of a good friend who can help keep you accountable. Money conversations are among the most difficult to have, but if these conversations can put you on a better financial path, they are absolutely worth it.

You can also reduce the amount you are spending on nonessential categories such as entertainment, new clothes, or eating out. Those are fantastic ways to save money and free up income to pay off debt and give to other people as well.

We would also suggest getting more intentional around paying off debt. In today's digital economy, the types of side hustles and extra jobs you could get are almost limitless. How badly do you want to get out of debt and have a better financial future? Remember that it's not just about you; it's also about your family and ultimately being a channel for a blessing.

Remember that your children are watching you.

As parents, we sometimes get so wrapped up in our own problems that we forget others are watching everything we say and do—especially our children! You may not think of yourself as a teacher, but you are. Your kids learn how to manage conflict, overcome problems, handle money, and more by looking at what we do (or don't do).

This should not feel intimidating. Instead, it's a blessing. We get to impact our kids not just during the time they live at home, but for the rest of their lives. If you are a grandparent, you can still continue to have a massive impact on your kids, and their kids as well. Everyone who comes behind you is watching and learning—not from what you say, but what you do. So take the opportunity to give and serve others, because that will set the example others will follow.

Keep an eternal perspective.

If you are a person of faith, you see everything you do in light of eternity. We are not just finite creatures who cease to exist one day. When we step through death's door, we simply step into a different type of existence. Knowing this impacts our daily lives in two ways.

First, it is a reminder that the frustrations we face on a daily basis are nothing compared to the expanse of eternity. As Paul wrote in 2 Corinthians 4:16–18, "So we do not lose heart. Though our outer self is wasting away, our inner self is being renewed day by day. For this light momentary affliction is preparing for us an eternal weight of glory beyond all comparison, as we look not to the things that are seen but to the things that are unseen. For the things that are seen are transient, but the things that are unseen are eternal."

Second, we know that our giving can have an impact far beyond what we experience on a daily basis. You can save a life, assist a friend in need, help build a house in another country, support your church and community, establish a better financial future for your family, and so much more when you give. You can *literally* change the world with your giving.

But if we want to change the world…it must begin with us. It begins with our attitude. It begins with stepping out of the familiar comfort of our everyday lives and taking a risk. It begins with caring enough to give, serve, and see things from an eternal perspective.

Keys to Performance-Driven Giving

In order to reduce indifference in your own heart, consider the following:

- Ask yourself honestly if you feel distracted. (The answer is probably yes!) What can you do to begin limiting these distractions? Even one small change can make a big difference.
- If you struggle with depression or other mental illness, what can you do to get healthier? Have you seen a professional?
- Assess your personal debt. Is it keeping you from giving as much as you could? How motivated do you feel to reduce your debt?

For Leaders: Five Symptoms of Indifference

Indifference can kill the effectiveness of a team and the organization's mission. However, it can be hard to spot, because it is not always as obvious as other destructive forces like gossip or dishonesty. However, it's just as destructive.

Indifference is like a virus. You can't see it directly, but you can see the symptoms. Below are five symptoms of indifference, along with questions to help you spot it.

1. **Conflict.** Does the person in question get along with others? How do they handle disagreements? Do they seem to lift up the team or tear down the team

2. **Negativity.** Do they have a positive attitude? How did they handle tough situations and disappointment? Does the emotional energy of the room go down when they walk in?

3. **Cynicism.** When they speak, do they have a sarcastic or bitter tone? Do they have a sense of hopefulness or despair toward the world in general?

4. **Anger.** Do they have a pleasant disposition, or do they make others uncomfortable? How do the team members respond to them? Do they handle setbacks well?

5. **Tribalism.** Are they a team player? Do they look out for the good of the whole group or just their own department or group? Do they see other coworkers as colleagues or competitors?

A Conversation with Andy Storch, Talent Development Consultant

In this chapter, you have learned to overcome indifference within yourself and others by increasing your passion, focus, connections, and other important qualities. We are thrilled to bring you this interview with Andy Storch, a business leader who embodies these qualities and much more.

Andy is a consultant, coach, speaker, and facilitator specializing in the talent development space. He is the author of *Own Your Career, Own Your Life: Stop Drifting and Take Control of Your Future* and the host of two podcasts: *Talent Development Hot Seat* and *Own Your Career*. And if that's not enough, Andy also heads up the Talent Development Think Tank Conference and Community.

We asked Andy to close out this chapter because he is the least indifferent person you will ever meet. Andy is full of passion and well known in entrepreneurial circles for being an amazing connector. We began our conversation with Andy by asking how we can better use social media to connect with people and add value.

We live in a time where we have the opportunity to have our voices heard by tons of people on social media. Our content can be available everywhere. That is the best way to connect because not everyone will go to conferences and events.

One important way you can be a giver on social media is to create content and engage with content. So instead of just promoting you and your brand or business all the time, find ways to give value to others. You can entertain them, inspire them, or educate them.

I like to create a lot of content that is inspiring for people in my network. I try to help them take some action that will improve their life. The easiest way for me to think about doing that is to focus on things I'm struggling with, or the things that help me.

Although we are all unique, most of us have very similar challenges. We all struggle with basically the same things. If I can share things I know are helpful for me, then I know they'll be helpful for other people. And I often hear from people who says, "Hey, thank you for sharing that. I needed to hear that today."

Another important way to use social media is to connect with people on a personal level. I do this all the time on LinkedIn and Facebook. I also have friends who do this really well on Instagram, where you can send people direct messages. You're just checking in with people and asking, "How are you doing? What are you working on? Is there any way I can support you?"

It's all about giving people value, whether it's advice, a referral, a recommendation, or something else that will help them. There are so many opportunities to do that, and a lot of that is facilitated by social media.

You can probably imagine our natural follow-up question: How do you keep from getting distracted by so many things going on and focus on what is most important? Andy shared some helpful words of advice.

I used to be a lot better at this. I still do a decent job, but there is always room for improvement. There are three factors to limiting distractions.

The first is planning my day and understanding what's important. What do I need to get done? What's on my schedule? Where do I have open time in my schedule? That's where I really value having a good journal. I use that to let me plan ahead and figure out when and how I'm going to do that.

The second is scheduling time for things that you need to get done. That can be global, like scheduling a block for getting things done that I said I was going to do. Or it can be really miniscule where every single little thing that you need to do, you put in your schedule. It might be things like calling the doctor at a certain time, talking to your spouse and having a conversation, or scheduling family game night or a date night.

The more you can schedule stuff and follow your schedule, the more effective and productive you're going to be.

The third piece is noticing how you are distracted by things and finding ways to cut down on those distractions. The biggest offender is the notifications on your phone and your computer. I really try to minimize those. As much as I love social media and am on it every day, I have all notifications from social media turned off on my phone.

Think about all the apps we use. Every single one of them is run by a company who has a group of employees whose single most important job is to make their app as addictive as possible so that you keep coming back to it again and again. If you want to take control of your time and your schedule, you've got to take control of how you operate.

Andy provides training for lots of companies and comes from a corporate background himself. It's easy to think that companies are only interested in profit, but he reminded us that there are a lot of great companies that care about their people. He had a few tips to put into practice.

I run a community for talent development professionals, and one of the topics on a recent call was, "How are you taking care of your people?" There is a study out there that shows 82 percent of employees say they are burned out or near burnout. How are we taking care of them?

The first piece is recognition. That's a really big one. Most people don't get the recognition or affirmation they really want. That is actually the number one thing many people care about: knowing their work is making a difference and getting those words of affirmation. Of course, the financial part of taking care of employees is a big deal, but this affirmation piece is very important.

There is also a lot of talk these days about how companies are helping people with health and wellness. They are incentivizing exercise, mindfulness, meditation, gratitude, and other related practices. Many companies are also looking for ways to give people more time off.

Another factor that will become more important in 2021 and beyond is the social justice movement. Forward-thinking companies are looking for ways to create more psychological safety and a more inclusive culture where people can show up, be themselves, and have equal opportunities so they're not discriminated against. Focusing on diversity, equity, and inclusion is huge right now.

Thanks, Andy! We are grateful for your leadership and efforts to help companies treat their people well.

Andy's website is https://andystorch.com. Make sure to check out his book, *Own Your Career, Own Your Life*, which will help you clarify your direction and seize the future. To listen to the entire interview, go to PerformanceDrivenThinking.com/Giving or scan the QR code to visit the page.

We also recommend connecting with Andy on social media:

Facebook: https://www.facebook.com/andystorch
LinkedIn: https://www.linkedin.com/in/andystorch
Twitter: https://twitter.com/AndyStorch
Instagram: https://www.instagram.com/andy_storch
Podcast: https://andystorch.com/podcast

PART 2
Branching Out

CHAPTER 5

Performance-Driven Giving in Your Personal Life

*"Fill yourselves first and then only
will you be able to give to others."*
—Augustine of Hippo

Each Saturday evening, Jewish families perform the Havdalah ceremony, which separates the Sabbath from the coming work week. Part of the ceremony involves a bottle of wine, a cup, and a saucer. They pour the wine into the cup, but when it is filled, they keep pouring until it overflows into the saucer below.

It might seem like a waste to keep pouring wine until it overflows, but the this is a symbol of the overflow our lives should produce. The ceremony illustrates the importance of serving from a full cup so that we can bless others out of the overflow.

In part 1, we spent four chapters establishing the roots of giving. Now we begin part 2, where we start to branch out and apply these principles to different areas of your life. In this chapter, we will focus on performance-driven giving in your personal life. We will discuss some ways to fill your cup and be able to give from the overflow.

Giving from an Overflowing Cup

We want you to give to others—that is what the whole book is about! But it must begin by giving to yourself. This is akin to putting on your own oxygen mask. If you are not taking care of yourself, you cannot help anyone else.

We will focus on three "cups" in your life that have a direct impact on your capacity to give: your health, finances, and spiritual growth. (We have already covered mindset in chapter 3, so we won't cover that again here.) For each of these three buckets, we will share why it is important to keep this cup filled, and a few ways to do it.

Cup 1: Health

Why It's Important

Imagine you are getting ready to buy a car. You're standing in the parking lot of a car dealership and see a new model that is exactly what you want. You walk around the car a few times, admiring the color and the design. You ask the salesperson to see the engine. As they pop the hood, you realize it doesn't have an engine!

This sounds like an unrealistic scenario, but this is how we often treat our bodies. We are more worried about our appearance and impressing others then we are concerned with the physical engine that keeps our lives running.

Your body is the engine that runs your life. Health and energy are related to giving because as we have mentioned before, you cannot give what you do not have. If you don't have the energy to function at your best, you will not have an overflow to offer others, whether it is serving, financial help, or giving in other ways.

One of the biggest objections we hear when we encourage people to get healthier is that they don't have time. But we would ask you this: If you die ten years earlier than you need to, was it worth the little bit of time you saved by not exercising?

Consider this as well: If you're not healthy and don't have energy, you are not operating at a high level. When you feel better and have more energy, you are more confident and productive. Think of exercise as an investment, not an expense. Treat your body like a business and take it as seriously as you take running your business or performing your job.

How to Keep Your Cup Filled

Obviously, health is a very personal matter, and everyone's situation is different. We don't presume to have a prescription that will work for everyone. However, these three strategies will work for almost everyone, no matter what the situation. These are a few critical areas that seem to trip people up.

- **Get enough sleep.** When you are not well-rested, everything in your life is more difficult. Your judgment is impaired, you are tired, and it compromises your immune system. In our world of social media and constant use of devices, it is easy to neglect sleep. However, it is one of the basic pillars of good health and success.
- **Exercise.** Everyone knows that we need to get exercise, but not as many people do it. The important thing is to do something that works for you and that you enjoy. Maybe it is hiking, bicycling, running, yoga, or something else you will do consistently.
- **Eat a healthy diet.** Of course this is easy to say, but harder to do in practice. Everyone knows eating less junk food and sugary snacks and more vegetables and lean meats will be good for you.
- **Manage stress.** As we mentioned in a previous chapter, mental health is a key area for health. We recommend engaging in practices such as meditation or devotional reading to help get you centered in your mental and spiritual life.

These are simply suggestions, and obviously you should consult a doctor before you start any nutrition or exercise plan. Furthermore, we hope you will do an honest assessment of where you are in your health. This is an area easy to ignore and sooner or later it will catch up with you. But the more attention we can give to our bodies and keep our life engine running smoothly, the more impact we can have, and the more we can give.

Cup 2: Finances

Why It's Important

This topic should not come as a surprise in a book about giving. But remember that giving is not just about money—it's about giving your life to serve others. And of course, money is part of that. If we use the analogy of the car from a few pages back, money is like the gasoline that fuels the car so we can keep moving forward. Without financial resources, we will soon be stuck on the side of road with no way to move forward.

As we mentioned in chapter 1, money is energy and we are channels of blessings for the money God gives to us. He wants to bless others through the blessings he has given us. God does his part, and we can do our part in becoming better stewards and earners.

On a practical level, money does only two things: It can be used to help others, and it gives you options in life. Both of those things are good. The more financially stable you are, the more you can do each of those things.

How to Keep Your Cup Filled

- **Get out of debt.** When you don't have debt, you can give more. Chances are high that you are dealing with debt. If so, don't beat yourself up over it. You cannot change the past, but you can decide today to create a better future for yourself. We recommend getting on Dave Ramsey's seven-step plan or some other financial program to help you deal with debt so you can free up more income.

- **Build giving into your budget.** Do you have a monthly budget where you allocate every dollar in advance? When you have a budget, it is not only a great stress relief, it's also a way to identify and control unnecessary expenses. We encourage you to make giving a regular part of your budget. Planned giving is a fantastic way to be more intentional about the resources you have.
- **Increase your earning capacity.** Both of us (Bobby and David) have built businesses and organizations, so we are fans of building something and creating your own future. We encourage you to think strategically about ways you can earn more income. It doesn't necessarily mean quitting your job. We recommend starting a side business of some kind. Check out Dan Miller's 48 Days material (https://48days.com) for lots of ideas on starting a side business.
- **Set giving goals.** If you're reading this book, you are probably already performing at a higher level. You're probably also used to setting goals and achieving them. This is a great way to increase your giving as well. You can set giving goals for the month or the year. Be sure to talk with your spouse so you get on the same page about your giving goals.

If this section makes you feel a little uncomfortable, that's okay. Money can be a touchy subject. But we want you to think bigger and know that any goal is possible if you think bigger.

Cup 3: Spiritual Growth

Why It's Important

We have used the metaphor of a tree several times in this book, and it's appropriate here as we talk about spiritual growth. You don't develop in your faith by accident. It takes intentional effort to grow into a "mighty oak" in your spiritual life. And if we can revisit the analogy of the car once again, your spiritual growth is like the navigation system that guides you on your journey.

You can have a working engine (health) and gasoline (money) that fuels the trip, but without navigation (spiritual growth), you will be lost, moving aimlessly through life. We suggest four important practices for spiritual growth below.

How to Keep Your Cup Filled

- **Read your Bible.** God's Word is the foundation on which our faith is built. If we want to maintain the foundation, we need to be in the Word on a regular basis. It doesn't mean you need to be a Bible scholar, but it does mean you have a genuine heart for seeking God's direction in your life. There are many ways to study the Bible, so we recommend asking a pastor or other spiritual leader for guidance in that area. Don't get hung up on one approach or method. Try a few different ones until you find an approach or system that works for you.

- **Pray.** It is rare to find someone who feels they are "good" at prayer. Why? Because we often associate prayer with flashy rhetoric and performance. But prayer is simply this: talking and listening to God. Prayer doesn't need to be a performance. It is just a time to talk to your heavenly Father, who loves and cares for you. You can pray in all kinds of ways, including talking out loud, journaling, going for a walk, or listening to worship music, just to name a few. In the times when you don't feel like praying, that is when you need to pray the most.

- **Get involved in a church.** It can be challenging to find a good church where you feel comfortable. That's why many people choose to skip church altogether. But remember, no church is perfect, because it's made up of people just like us. A good church is a wonderful place to find support for your faith and a community of people who love God and serve others.

- **Participate in a small group.** Small groups can take many different forms. Some focus on studying curriculum, some focus on serving, and others just like to fellowship. However, the one they have in common is that people are gathering together to boost their faith. If your church doesn't have a small group program, take the initiative and start your own. You can invite people to join you in person or online for study, fellowship, or service.

These three cups—health, finances, and spiritual growth—are vital for your personal growth and giving. Don't neglect them. When your cup overflows, you are in a much better position to honor God and bless others.

Leading Your Family in Giving

Now that we have established the importance of giving from an overflowing cup, we want to help you lead your family in giving. This is where the rubber meets the road! If you cannot lead your family in this process, how can you lead a team or organization?

When you have laid a strong foundation by keeping your cups filled in the three areas mentioned above, you are more capable of leading your family. We first give to God, then ourselves, then our family. It is easy to neglect family relationships because they often don't complain and just accept things the way they are.

But this is why it's so important to care for our families well: Those relationships can go sour for a long time before we wake up and realize anything is wrong. You can have a great job and perhaps make a lot of money. You can even give generously to causes and organizations. But if your family is falling apart, you have failed in your most important job.

Let's discuss some strategies for creating a culture of giving in your marriage and in your parenting.

Building a Giving Marriage

Countless books have been written on how to maintain a healthy marriage. We wish we had the space to dedicate a whole chapter to the importance of giving in keeping your marriage healthy. However, we will hit a few critical areas that will help you strengthen the most important relationship in your life.

Resolving Conflict

If you ask any newly married couple if they believe they will always get along, they may naïvely say yes. But they will soon discover that conflict happens! It's something we deal with throughout our whole marriage. Conflict resolution is one of the most important skills we can develop in any relationship, particularly our marriage.

When you have a disagreement with your spouse, how do you resolve the conflict? Do you tend to shut down and go silent, hoping that the other party comes to you? Or do you take initiative and try to work it out as soon as you can?

There is a great deal of wisdom in Paul's words from Ephesians 4:26: "Be angry and do not sin; do not let the sun go down on your anger." One of the most giving actions we can take in our marriage is to take initiative in resolving conflicts.

Being Thoughtful

Another way to give is by showing generosity and thoughtfulness. This comes easy for newlyweds. They are excited about their new relationship and sometimes go to great lengths to express their love for each other. But as we get older, we are not as thoughtful. We just assume our spouse knows we love them.

What is something thoughtful you have done for your husband and wife lately? Maybe it was a small gift, date night, or making a special surprise meal. A great resource for understanding her spouse is Gary Chapman's book *The Five Love Languages*. If you don't know your spouse's love language, we encourage you to check it out, because it can help you express love to them in a way they appreciate the most.

Setting Goals

We also recommend making sure you are on the same page with your goals. Whether your goals are related to finances, relationship, career, parenting, or another area, they are easy to neglect in a marriage. When you are busy raising kids, you are consumed with everyday life. The years go by, then all of a sudden you find yourself with an empty nest and no clear pathway forward in your marriage. You might even find that you have become two completely different people. Many couples get divorced soon after their kids leave home.

Take some time to sit down with your spouse and think about your goals. Do you want the same things? Are you moving in the same direction? If you have kids at home, hire a babysitter and take an evening to go out to dinner and discuss your goals. It is one of the best investments you can make in your marriage. If you keep your own cups filled, you can show up to marriage in a healthy, energetic, and devoted manner. You can be the leader and giver you need to be.

Dealing with a Difficult Marriage

However, you might be in a difficult marriage. What if your spouse is not supportive? What if there is deep-seated conflict and you are not on the same page with your goals? Or what if your spouse is not supportive of your desire to give?

Remember that you cannot change someone else. You can only change yourself. As much as you may want to change your spouse's behavior or priorities, you cannot force them. You can only be a model for the kind of life you want to live.

That may sound disappointing at first, but it's actually a blessing. Not being responsible for anyone else's mindset takes the pressure off. You can only be responsible for your own attitude and outlook. Make sure you are modeling a serving, giving, generous, thoughtful spirit. This is easier said than done!

Remember that change takes time as well. People don't change overnight. Think of a habit that you successfully changed. It probably took a few tries and took longer and a lot more effort than you thought. In our fast-paced modern world, we get impatient with ourselves and others. It takes time to develop new habits and goals.

If you're in a less-than-ideal marriage, this is also a great time to ask if you have expressed your desires openly and clearly to your spouse. Sometimes we think we have communicated well, when in fact the other person has no idea what we want or how we feel. It is always good to have an open conversation about your relationship, your needs, and your goals.

When it comes to giving, if your spouse is not on board, you can always give from your personal funds. If you're in an extreme situation where you do not have access to money in your marriage, you can serve and give in other ways. Remember that you are never powerless in the situation. You always have options. Your current situation may hold the key to overcoming it.

Raising Kids Who Are Givers

Many of the same principles that we mentioned about marriage apply to parenting. Obviously, they are two different things, but they both involve your relationship with the most important people in your life. We suggest a few steps to help you raise kids who are generous givers.

The most important thing is simply modeling the behavior that you want to see. You can lecture all you want, but ultimately kids do what kids see. Are you being a giver? Are you serving? Are you generous? Are you handling your money correctly? This is the number one principle of teaching—modeling the behavior that we want to see.

Another great way to help your kids become givers is to offer them opportunities to give and serve. This could take on many different forms depending on your situation. There are the obvious opportunities such as church, community organizations, and school. But other giving opportunities come up in the everyday situations of life, like assisting a homeless person or helping a friend who has an urgent need.

Sometimes we think kids are too young to learn, and it is easy to short-change them. Kids love to help and be involved. Are you exposing them to opportunities all around you so they can develop their giving muscle?

As we mentioned earlier, change takes time. If your kids are a little older, and they are already established in their habits or lack thereof, it may take some time to turn those habits around. But your kids are never too old for you to impact them. Even well into their adulthood, when they become parents, you can set a powerful example by continuing to give and show them that the giving life is the only one worth living.

Taking a Leap of Faith

I (David) would like to close out this chapter by sharing that illustrates the importance of using as a family around giving.

There was a time in my life when my family was not tithing to our church. We felt like we couldn't afford to do it because we had so much financial stress on us. As the breadwinner in the family, I was especially concerned about making ends meet and making sure we had enough money in the bank.

One day we were sitting in church and the pastor was teaching about tithing. He challenged everyone there to begin giving 10 percent or more right then and said that if they remained faithful in tithing for ninety days and don't see an increase in your life, he would refund 100 percent of their money.

I had a sinking feeling in my gut because I knew we had not been giving. I knew that giving blesses other people but during that time in our lives, I was hesitant to do it. My wife looked at me as if to say, "We can't afford it." But in that moment I felt that couldn't afford not to give it a try. So we took the challenge.

Before the ninety days was up, we had a $12,000 check show up in the mail out of the blue. It for an excess payment on a life insurance policy. The amount was exactly what we needed at the time, and there was no way I could have earned that extra money in three months.

I reached out to the pastor to share my story and said, "I'm not going to be one of the people who asks for a refund!" He said nobody else had asked for a refund, either. That experience brought us back to tithing. There have been times that were stressful, but the money has always been there for what we needed. God has always provided. This challenge put me back on the straight and narrow and showed me the power of giving to change your life.

This is an easy chapter to skip. Since you are a performance-driven person, you probably want to focus on strategies for business of personal growth. You want to impact the world, and that is a good thing!

However, the biggest impact we can make is first within our own life, then in the lives of our spouse and kids. Mother Teresa said, "It's not how much we give but how much love we put into giving." In our pursuit of impacting the community and world, let's not forget that the most important place to display this love is right within our own homes.

Keys to Performance-Driven Giving

In order to improve giving in your personal life, consider the following:

1. How are you doing with each of the three "cups" we mentioned—health, finances, and spiritual growth? Do any of those cups feel empty? Why? What actions can you take in the next to start filling it?

2. If you are married, do you and your spouse have the same giving goals? Do you ever talk about giving?

3. If you have children, what are some ways you are teaching them about giving? What do you wish your parents would have taught you?

Head, Heart, Hands: Three Ways People Connect with Giving

An important truth to remember when it comes to giving is that people have different motivations. What motivates or moves us may not motivate or move someone else. This is also true within our families. You may love your spouse and kids (and hopefully do!), but different personalities connect with giving for different reasons.

The head, heart, hands framework below is a helpful tool for understanding how others connect with giving, whether it's in your family, community, or workplace.

- **Head (Thinking).** These are people who like to study, analyze, and review data. They love reports, charts, graphs, and systematic ways to look at everything related to giving.

- **Heart (Emotions).** These are people who give based on what moves them emotionally. They especially connect with stories, videos, pictures, and the human side of giving.

- **Hands (Action).** These are people who like to get things done. If you offer a mission trip to build a house, they will be the first to sign up. They feel satisfied when they see tangible progress toward a giving goal.

A Conversation with Vincent Pugliese, Entrepreneur and Coach

In this chapter, we have focused on giving in your personal life. We have looked at a multitude of ways to become a stronger giver by focusing on your health, finances, marriage, family, and other areas. We are thrilled to conclude this chapter with a friend who models the themes we have been talking about: Vincent Pugliese.

Vincent was a professional photojournalist for twenty-three years. He has photographed four US presidents and nearly every major sporting event. His work has been published in most major newspapers, magazines, and online publications throughout the world.

Vincent now coaches and leads small business owners and freelancers towards a life of time, money, and location freedom through his Total Life Freedom mastermind and community. You can read his story in his excellent book *Freelance to Freedom: The Roadmap for Creating a Side Business to Achieve Financial, Time, and Life Freedom.*

Vincent is truly a giver in every aspect of his life, and we began our conversation by asking, "How do you make giving and generosity a bigger part of your marriage."

It's a great question. I could give a very typical answer, such as "Be more thoughtful or pay more attention." And that's great advice. I don't like to turn everything back to business, but what I have learned is that by freeing up time and money, I could become a better husband and father.

It sounds kind of selfish, but when you free up more of your time, you can run a better business and become a more generous spouse and parent. That only happened because we focused on the business to build the life we wanted. Now I can go for a three-hour bike ride and can have these long conversations. Or my wife can go shopping or buy groceries and we don't have to worry what the bill is. The stress level comes way down.

I wasn't able to be generous when I was strapped. I wasn't able to be attentive when I was without money or time. Building the business was not about the money; it was about the freedom that allowed us to have a better family.

We asked Vincent to follow up by sharing some things that he and his wife, Elizabeth, do to try to help their three boys be more generous.

Kids are naturally selfish, right? I was that way when I was younger. We all were. So we are constantly having conversations about how to best help them learn to be generous.

We want them to know that giving their time and money is very important. Right now, our sons are fifteen, thirteen, and nine. When we are home, we go to the homeless shelters and they help out by making lunches, taking the garbage out, and sweeping the floors. They need to understand they have a very good life. A key component to appreciating the things you have in life and being a good contributor to society is to be generous.

Christmas is one of those times where it's typically all about "What am I getting?" One Christmas a few years ago, I wanted to shift the focus from what they were getting to what they could give. We started a tradition where we go out, take a lot of money and candy canes, and go to poor neighborhoods.

We just gave out money and at first the kids were like, "What are we doing?" But then they loved it. And by the third year, our son Andrew came up to me and said, "Dad, I actually like Christmas Eve better than I like Christmas." That was huge.

I'll never forget one Christmas Eve when we were in Pittsburgh. We came out of church and went to do the money thing. We saw a woman in a wheelchair. It was freezing and she had no shoes on. It was the bad part of town, almost eight thirty at night.

We pulled up next to her and gave her the $20 with a candy cane. She was so thankful she was crying. We kept stopping every ten feet, giving her more and more. We just wanted to help.

On that same night, we went to another bad area of town. We pulled over to give a woman some money. She started crying and said, "Nobody's ever given me a Christmas gift before." And for the kids to hear that was amazing. I don't think it always sinks in immediately. But the repetition and consistency help them to think that way.

What a great story! While giving is important, and it's obviously the theme of this book, it's also important to receive the gifts others want to give you. We asked Vincent how he stays open to receiving...and he didn't mince any words.

I'm bad at it. I don't like it. I don't know why. I'm just not good at it.

For those of us who enjoy giving, it's easy to push off receiving, even in terms of receiving compliments. But it's not good because it doesn't give honor to the people who are giving it to you. If I gave you a compliment and you didn't receive it, it would actually make me feel worse.

A lot of us are individualistic and we want to get it done ourselves. So receiving often feels like charity. We don't want charity, but people love to give and we're robbing them of the opportunity to give by doing that. I don't have a great answer for you, except that I struggle with it, like a lot of people.

Thanks, Vincent! We appreciate your honesty, as well as the tremendous value you add to entrepreneurs and business leaders through your work and your life.

Vincent's website is https://totallifefreedom.com. Make sure to check out his inspiring book, *Freelance to Freedom*, which will help you create a side business that gives you freedom in your time, money, and life. To listen to the entire interview, go to PerformanceDrivenThinking.com/ Giving or scan the QR code to visit the page.

We also recommend connecting with Vincent on social media:

Facebook: https://www.facebook.com/vincent.pugliese.16
LinkedIn: https://www.linkedin.com/in/vincent-pugliese-3955321a
Podcast: https://totallifefreedom.com

CHAPTER 6

Performance-Driven Giving in Business

Your true worth is determined by how much more you give in value than you take in payment.
—Bob Burg and John David Mann

Today, we don't think much about railroads. It was the primary mode of mass transportation in the US for nearly a hundred years, but it has mostly been overtaken by subways, cars, semis, and airplanes.

However, there was a time when railroad magnates were some of the richest men in the country. One such man was E. H. Harriman, whose family came to the US from London in 1795. His father was a minister, but he chose a different path and instead went into finance. After a stint on Wall Street, he married into a family that was involved in the railroad business, and he soon bought his own rail lines. Eventually he controlled the Union Pacific Railroad.

But Harriman wasn't in it for the money. Rather, his main concern was what he could accomplish with money. He famously said, "Great wealth is an obligation and responsibility. Money must work for the country." In addition, he once said, "I have never cared for money except as a power to put into work. What I enjoy most is the power of creation, getting into partnership with nature and doing good, helping to feed man and beast, and making everybody and everything a little better and happier."

In our previous book, we wrote that the best measurement of a business is performance-driven thinking. The ultimate expression of good thinking is giving. The purpose of business is not just to make a profit, but to do good in the world. The result is that we do well by doing good.

In this chapter we'll look at several aspects of performance-driven giving in business. We'll begin with a look at giving in business from a leader's perspective, followed by some thoughts for team members.

We'll conclude this chapter with some thoughts for entrepreneurs. They are in business as well, although their business looks different. There are increasingly more entrepreneurs and small business owners, so we want to make sure they are included as well.

Fundamentals for Business Leaders

There is a lot to take into consideration when you are the leader of an organization, no matter how big or small it is. We will keep this simple by covering a few fundamental principles of giving for business leaders.

Commit to giving because it is the right thing to do.

This is the most fundamental principle of all. You must believe in the power of giving, and you must commit to it because in your heart you feel it is what you must do.

Yes, giving is good for business, but that is not the primary reason we give. We give because it is how we honor God and express love to people. When it comes down to it, there is no other reason. Everything else that comes from giving, any other benefits, are the consequences of giving, not the motive. We give because we want to do good, not just look good.

We know that not everyone comes to giving from a faith perspective. If you have read thus far in the book but you're not a person of faith, we commend you! We come at giving from a point of view of faith, and we believe we have a corporate responsibility to tithe.

That sounds radical in an age where many businesses are struggling just to pay the bills, but we feel it is a big reason why God has blessed us and our organizations have been successful.

Embrace the idea that giving is good for business.

This sounds like we are rejecting the altruism of giving, but let's face it: Giving is never an entirely altruistic enterprise. That is a naïve understanding of giving. People sometimes reject giving because they look at it as a one-way street, but it's not.

Giving is a symbiotic partnership where everyone benefits because of the exchange of goodwill and value. Giving spreads abundance for everyone, not just the person who receives the giving. This does not go against what we just said about our motive for giving—that never changes. But we must face the reality that giving does bring business benefits.

Here is an interesting principle: if there are two identical businesses, 90 percent of customers will subconsciously do business with the one that has a public giving campaign. Why? People want to be associated with that. They want to do business with people who are doing in the world. This has been a big part of business since the 1980s.

When you give, you don't need to self-righteous about it or make a grandiose show of it. Just understand that people want to participate in doing good. People want to see positive change in the world, and if they perceive you are helping others, they want to be a part of that. They want to see the impact of your giving and feel good about doing business with you.

Select key partners who align with your mission and values.

We'll talk more about a framework for selecting where to give in chapter 10. But for now, we want to mention a couple of important things related to partnerships.

First, giving is not just about charity to a needy organization. That is a simplistic understanding of giving. Giving is about partnerships, relationships, and collaboration. It's about developing mutual good and adding value to each other.

Second, we don't believe in competition. We believe in collaboration. You might think that sounds nice but wonder how that works in real life. We see "competitors" as people who can be a gateway to a collaboration of some kind. You can be in the same business as someone else, but you are not the same business. You each have unique strengths, markets, and missions. Because no two businesses are exactly the same, there is no competition.

At Morgan James, we view all our constituents as valued partners in our mission to bring great books into the world. Bookstores are of course a highly valued partner in our business. We give our authors a higher royalty than is typical for traditional book publishers. We have also just begun offering group health insurance to our authors, something that is unheard of in the publishing world. And we have already mentioned our partnership with Habitat for Humanity.

Collaboration is all about recognizing people who are smarter than you or have some other advantage that can help you be more successful. Likewise, you have unique strengths that others can benefit from as well.

Bake giving into your products and services.

The vast majority of businesses miss this important principle of "baking" giving into what they do. It doesn't mean that giving has to be their main business or message. It just means finding ways to embody the message of giving into some of the things you offer in your business.

For example, in 2016 we published the *Do Good Stuff: Journal* by Joel Comm. The book was created to help people keep track of their good deeds and motivate them to do more. Whether lending a helping hand, building up others, taking care of family or friends, donating time or talents to a worthwhile cause, or being a leader, the *Do Good Stuff: Journal* was designed to help readers make a difference they could document in the book. Ten percent of all profits from the journal go directly to WaterIsLife.com, a nonprofit organization dedicated to bringing clean water solutions to developing countries.

What are some ways you can build giving directly into your business? You don't need to be a publisher to do this. You might offer a free community event, consultations or coaching, workshops, or many other ways to add value by giving.

Show people how their giving is impacting lives.

Older generations grew up in a time when most people trusted institutions. Government leaders, educators, pastors, and business leaders were generally seen as trustworthy, upstanding figures who were doing good in the world and benefiting society. My, how times have changed!

Trust in organizations and institutions has eroded over the last few decades. We no longer automatically trust authority figures. In fact, people are more likely to mistrust them until they have a reason not to do so. This is especially true for younger generations such as Millennials and Gen Zers. They have heard horror stories of authority figures abusing their power, stealing from nonprofits, and getting away with bad behavior.

Regardless of what type of organization or business you are leading, you must work hard to develop trust and show how your giving is impacting human lives. Younger generations no longer take anything at face value. They want to be involved and know where their money and resources are going. They want to see data, stats, newsletters, and other info that helps them makes informed decisions and decide when and how to give.

Millennials and Gen Zers also have less money. Many of them are still living with their parents. It is easy for them to be cynical because they don't see how their small gifts can make a difference. By using social media, video, podcasts, and other types of content marketing, you can show them exactly how their gifts translate into impacting lives.

One such company that puts these five principles into practice is Askinosie Chocolate, based in Springfield, Missouri. Shawn Askinosie was a successful criminal defense attorney who wanted to make a shift in his career. In a flash of insight, he decided that he wanted to be a chocolate maker. After bringing his skills as an attorney to bear on his newfound interest, he found himself in the Amazon just a few months later learning about chocolate firsthand from the farmers who produced the cocoa beans.

But Shawn didn't want to just create another chocolate company. On his company website, he writes, "And off we went, doing what we do, meeting and working with farmers and communities from four continents to tackle the mysteries, magic and heartache of trying to make perfect chocolate, from profit sharing to packaging our beautiful bars, for a long while having no idea whether we would one day make money, or were sinking our life savings into a shiny stainless-steel tank of brown goo."

He continues, "Having built the business from scratch, I can confidently say the greatest opportunity and challenge has been weaving social responsibility into everything we do; it's not just a buzzword, it's who we are. Askinosie Chocolate was born committed to fairness, sustainability, minimal environmental impact, and community enhancement. Those commitments will be in place as long as the company is. We're dedicated not just to making the best quality chocolate you can buy, but to making it in such a way that the more you learn about it, the better you feel about it."

You can more about Shawn's story at the Askinosie Chocolate website (https://askinosie.com) or in Shawn's book, *Meaningful Work: A Quest to Do Great Business, Find Your Calling, and Feed Your Soul.*

Giving as a Team Member

Now that we have taken a look at how leaders can incorporate giving into their business more effectively, let's turn our attention to how employees and team members can give.

The biggest reason people are sometimes resistant to giving is that they perceive giving is all about money. Of course, we have seen so far in this book that giving really concerns all of life—your family, your spirituality, your work, your health, and of course your finances.

So in that spirit, we thought it would be helpful to list a few ways to give without using money. These are a few simple suggestions for ways to support what your company or organization is doing by giving your time, talent, and treasure.

Get involved in teaching and training.

If you enjoy creating content, this is a great opportunity to serve your team. Every organization needs training on many different topics, and every person is an expert at something. You can write, create podcasts, put together workshops, create videos, or explore many other ways to train others in skills they can use for your organization.

Mentor and coach others.

Are there team members who are less experienced than you or need help in a certain area? The answer is almost certainly a yes, because everyone should constantly be on a growth trajectory. You don't need to necessarily have a formal mentoring or internship arrangement, although those can be helpful. You can informally work with others to give you time and knowledge so they can grow.

Remember you are part of the sales team.

Every person at your organization is in sales. You may or may not have a sales team, but every team member has responsibility to help sell the company to others. Everyone is in marketing.

You can volunteer to help in a specific capacity, or you simply view yourself as a goodwill ambassador for your team. You can take to social media to talk positively, wear company merchandise or logos, or help in an endless number of ways to get the word out about your products or services.

Ask how you can help.

This is such a simple concept, yet it is rarely practiced. When is the last time you directly asked another department member how you can help? You might be surprised at the answers. Even if they don't respond with something specific, they will appreciate the fact that you were thoughtful enough to ask.

Listen to others.

We live in a highly distracted world, and our listening skills as a society seem to be disappearing a little more each year. But by practicing empathetic listening, you can transform someone's day. When you listen, people feel heard. They feel validated and affirmed. This is a wonderful way you can give and contribute to a culture of caring within our organization.

Remember people's birthdays and anniversaries.

When we think of giving, we tend to focus on the big items, like donating money or volunteering for a noteworthy project. But people appreciate being acknowledged, and a great way to do this is to remember days that are special to them. This is no less a form of giving—in fact, it is one of the highest forms simply because most people don't pay attention to the little things.

Volunteer to help.

This can be a variety of things depending on the situation. Simply put, when leaders ask for volunteers, do your best to help. It may not be something you enjoy, but the fact that you engaged and participated will mean a lot, and also set you apart as a leader who cares about people and supports others outside your official responsibilities.

Be positive.

It seems like such a simple thing, doesn't it? "Be positive." But it's so powerful because so few people are intentionally positive. Establishing a great culture of giving is not just the responsibility of the leader or administrators. It's everyone's responsibility.

Do your best to be easy to work with, compliant with requests, and supportive of decisions, even though you might choose something different. One positive attitude can make a world of difference.

Be excellent at your job.

Most people only give what is expected of them, and nothing more. However, excellence demands that we do our best and give a little extra because it's the right thing to do. Excellence can mean different things to different people, but it's essentially doing the best you are capable of.

It means showing up mentally and emotionally and putting in our best effort day after day. It seems like an obvious thing to do, but it's not for most people, which makes it that much more urgent for you.

Give credit where credit is due.

A lot of good work in organizations (and other places) goes unnoticed because most people don't take the time to recognize and celebrate it. You don't need to be the main leader to do this. You simply have to practice "positive gossip" about others and help spread the word about their good deeds.

Stay mentally and emotionally healthy.

We talked about this in a previous chapter, but it bears repeating here. One of the most important ways you can be a giver is to maintain your capacity to give. That means having the energy and focus to be aware of opportunities to give. If you are always tired and don't have the energy to engage with people, you will only be operating at partial capacity.

Keep a clean environment.

This point is almost embarrassing because we're all adults here, right? That may be true, but many adults don't act very mature when it comes to simple cleanliness.

Is your office or area messy and cluttered? Do you pick up after yourself? Do you throw away a piece of trash you see on the ground? Do you wash the dishes you used in the company kitchen? If not, be mindful that simple things like this are a great way to establish a culture of service and simply make life easier for your team members.

Be a connector.

Every person you know is looking for someone to help with a particular need. It may be personal or related to business, but that's not the point. The main idea is that you know people who can help others in your network. Be on the lookout for ways you can connect people who need each other. This is an amazing way you can give your attention and your network to others who need it.

Giving as an Entrepreneur or Small Business Owner

If you have read this far into the chapter, it may feel like we have mostly been addressing leaders and team members of organization that have a couple dozen employees or more. While that has certainly been on our minds, we know that businesses come in all shapes and sizes.

In this section, we offer some tips for solo entrepreneurs, freelancers, and small business owners. There are many ways you can give without busting your budget.

Give referrals.

We do business with people we know, like, and trust. If we make a referral, we are passing on that trust to the person we are referring. The person being referred comes to the potential client with some trust already in their pocket, assuming the relationship we have with the potential client is good.

All three people win when you make a good referral. The person you are referring gets potential business, the person you're referring them to gets someone they trust, and you win because now both people trust you even more, plus you have done some good in the world. And it might come back to you interesting ways in the future.

Promote other businesses and causes.

There are endless ways to do cross promotions. When you get creative with your marketing and social media, you can find some interesting ways to mention other businesses and causes in a natural way that does not feel forced.

If you do not feel creative when it comes to social media, we recommend going through a bit of training on how to do this well. You can also follow a few businesses or brands that you like and model what they are doing.

You might ask, "Does this really count as giving? It sounds like good old-fashioned networking to me." And that is probably true. But there is a difference between promotion for selfish reasons and doing it because you believe in what you are promoting and how that business or cause is helping other people.

The bottom line is that when you help others, it does come back to you, but that is not the main reason to do it. We do it because it's the right way to do business and operate in a world where we benefit from great partnerships.

Give more in value than you are paid for.

This sounds like a simple business principle, and in a way, it is. But it bears mentioning here because so many people just view business as an exchange of value for money. We believe the best way to do business is to give more in value than you are receiving in payment. Yes, this is good business, but it's also giving because business is ultimately all about creating value for others.

Does this mean you give away the farm? No, it doesn't mean doing a bunch of work for free. It just means that you go the extra mile to ensure your work is excellent, you do little favors, and you think about what the client or customer needs before they ask. It's really just a mindset where you're hyper-aware of serving people, and you go above and beyond to make sure they are served well.

Volunteer.

If your budget is tight, you can volunteer for any number of causes, charities, or organizations. If you are running a solo or small business, it probably feels like time is the last thing you have. But you don't need a massive amount of time to make a big impact. Even just one or two hours per month can help establish a relationship that will create much bigger opportunities for giving down the road.

If finances are a concern (and let's face it, they are always a concern), you can also do pro bono work for causes you support. Maybe it's writing, web design, graphic design, coaching, or something else. If you're in the early stages of building your business, this can also be a great way to build your network and skills, so it's a double win.

Smart small.

You might feel overwhelmed at all the suggestions and ideas. However, we don't want you to come away thinking you have to put all these ideas into practice in order to give in a meaningful way. Start small and then give, volunteer, and serve as you are able.

In chapter 9, we will dive more into the concept of starting small. But here is the gist of it: Good things take time to grow. Nothing important was built quickly. Everything begins as an idea, as a concept, as a simple urge to help in some small way. Don't despise small beginnings. It's not how you start; it's how you finish.

Create great content.

This might sound self-serving, and we wouldn't blame you for feeling that way. After all, when you create content, it helps promote your business, right? That is correct, but good content also serves people who might never do business with you. In the mix of content marketing, content is half of the game.

What does "good content" mean, anyway? It means material that helps people solve a problem or inspires them in some way. It means you are in tune with your audience and you want to serve them. It means you work hard on the content to ensure that it's valuable on its own, rather than just a marketing piece.

As we've looked at different aspects of performance-driven giving in the world of business, here is the big takeaway we want you to think about: The final result of giving in business is that you can have greater impact in the community, more profitability, and a better team. Who wouldn't want that?

Giving is a gateway to all kinds of great things—not just because of the act of giving, but because the thinking that led you to give in the first place is also the kind of thinking that will help you succeed in business.

Keys to Performance-Driven Giving

In order to begin giving more effectively in your business, consider the following:

1. Review the list of reasons why most businesses don't give. Do you relate to any of these? Have you ever served with an orga-

nization or company that did not give? Were these reasons valid in that context?

2. Partnerships are a vital way to give more deeply and establish relationships with people who can elevate your giving. What current partnerships do you have that allow you give more? What opportunities do you have to partner with others?

3. Do you have giving goals as a team member, entrepreneur, or business leader? Are the goals specific enough that you could articulate them to another person? Are the goals realistic and meaningful to you personally?

Answering the Objections

When it comes to giving, leaders and team members alike will naturally have lots of questions and even objections. Here are some of the most common objections we hear, along with our responses.

Objection: My board or investors do not support giving.

Our first response would be "Are you sure?" Perhaps they don't support a specific type of giving, or a giving plan was presented to them in the wrong way. We have rarely found a board or a group of leaders that did not enthusiastically support giving when it was presented to them as a way to boost morale, build partnerships, increase goodwill, and ultimately make you more profitable.

Objection: The economy is too unstable to start giving right now.

There is never really a good time to initiate a change that might feel risky. The truth is that risk has a lot more to do with your industry and your particular organization than it does with the whole economy. Don't believe everything you hear in the media.

When you follow the principles we have laid out in this book for establishing a giving program, you can do it slowly while mitigating risk. In fact, when you build partnerships through giving, this only strengthens your overall market position.

Objection: Expenses keep going up, and I don't want to risk our financial margin.

It is true that some expenses, such as health insurance, keep going up. We feel your pain on that one. But remember that giving is not just about donating money to a cause; it can be done many ways without using business funds.

When Morgan James started working with Habitat for Humanity, we didn't have any extra money to give. Instead, we promoted Habitat as a partner, which is a practice we continue today. Every one of our books features Habitat for Humanity on both the copyright page and the back cover. There are many ways to give, and money is just one.

As you develop partnerships for giving, more people will hear about you and want to work with you. This will hopefully increase your exposure and lead to growth in your company, which will allow you to begin giving financially.

Objection: I don't know how to structure giving into my company.

We suggest beginning with a non-monetary partnership, as with our relationship with Habitat. This involves very little structure and doesn't even have to be a major official policy. Just take small steps and find a great partner. Then as you get more experience, reach out to other companies who have more structured partnerships and get insights on how they structure this into their organization.

A Conversation with Bea Boccalandro, Speaker and Advisor on Work Purpose

In this chapter, we have tried to help you look at giving in a business context from several points of view. No matter what type of organization or company you serve, and no matter your role, these principles will help you become a stronger giver.

We are thrilled to feature our friend Bea Boccalandro in this interview. Bea is the author of *Do Good at Work: How Simple Acts of Social Purpose Drive Success and Wellbeing*. She advises business leaders on igniting social purpose in the workplace and helps workers end their workday knowing they made a difference.

Bea is also the founder and president of VeraWorks, a global firm that helps businesses implement and measure the impact of pursuing social purpose. She is an expert on job purposing, a proven way to heighten workplace productivity, satisfaction, and well-being. That's why we are grateful to share this interview with Bea on giving in a business context.

We began the conversation by asking Bea about the connection between clarity of purpose and giving.

Many people find it surprising that we can have a life deeply enriched by giving without having a clearly defined life purpose. When it comes to the benefits of giving, lacking a life purpose is not a setback.

There's a distinction between life purpose and social purpose. Many people suggest that we should be clear on our life's purpose, on the singular and unique way we make our days on earth meaningful. They say that doing the reflection work to define our personal life's purpose (beyond self-serving aims) makes us healthier, happier, and more successful. Research shows that this is true. But what most people don't know is that there's a simpler, and just as fulfilling, path to those benefits. This shortcut, or "purpose hack," as I like to refer to it, is social purpose. Social purpose is defined as contributing to others or to a soci-

etal cause, however we can, whenever we can. Living in accordance to the universal, versatile, and broad social purpose gives us the same sense of meaning—and triggers the same health, happiness, and success benefits—that living in accordance to a unique, narrow, and specific life purpose does. And it's a lot less work!

If you happen to have a specific life purpose statement taped to your bathroom mirror that says, "I bring hope parents with autistic children" or "I solve difficult problems to help humanity progress," that's great! If it's working, don't tear it down. But posting "Today I will somehow contribute to someone or to a societal cause" is just as good—and it's plug and play, no deep reflection or wordsmithing necessary!

We followed up by asking Bea how a lack of purpose affects people's motivation and attitude.

Research shows that if what you are doing has social purpose woven into it, your motivation goes way up. Some examples of work with social purpose woven into it might be sitting down to work on a spreadsheet for a nonprofit cause or lowering the stress of a co-worker on your sales team by helping them complete a task they found frustrating.

But really, making any type of meaningful contribution to another or to the world works. Doing so will facilitate getting into a state of flow. You'll work longer and harder without knowing that you're doing so. And studies suggest the quality of your work goes up. You are essentially hardwired to fire on all cylinders when pursuing social purpose. Purpose and motivation are very closely linked.

Once people have a strong social purpose in place, leaders can feed into that purpose by reinforcing generosity and creating a giving culture. Bea offered some great suggestions for how leaders can give to their team members.

Luckily, there are many ways to infuse work with social purpose. My book has over a hundred examples. Leaders can ignite their work with social purpose by making sure team members receive mentoring to support their careers, for example. They can also adopt the practice of always asking quiet meeting participants to share their thoughts, especially since these individuals are overwhelmingly women and minorities. This simple tactic, therefore, makes the workplace more equitable.

Of course, there are also audacious ways to infuse work with social purpose. In the US, we have a living wage issue. It's possible, likely in some circumstances, that your full-time workers aren't able to provide properly for their children, to give them a life that will allow them to thrive as adults. If you want to go all out, a way of infusing your business with social purpose might be to make the minimum wage at your company, say, $80,000 a year.

You can also make housecleaning a free employee perk, which is an especially powerful aid to single mothers on your team. Or you can commit your company to making 50 percent of new hires be disabled military veterans. There are so many ways to give to team members. A lot of leaders are stepping up to the plate. All of the examples I give in the book are real. It's awe inspiring to see so many leaders find ways to contribute to their team members.

Our final question focused on whether there was a connection between a company's culture of giving and its financial success. The answer surprised us.

Yes, there is a connection between a culture of giving and financial success. One study discovered that organizations with a giving culture perform 42 percent better than the market.

Another group of researchers did a five-year study on which companies grow. To their own surprise, social purpose showed up as one of the biggest drivers of growth. There absolutely is a connection.

At first these findings sound surprising to most of us. But when you consider what we were talking about earlier, the link between social purpose and motivation and performance, how could a culture of giving not drive growth?

Thanks, Bea! We are grateful you have shared your wisdom on how business leaders can become more effective performance-driven givers.

Bea's website is https://www.beaboccalandro.com. Make sure to check out her amazing book, *Do Good at Work*, which will help your organization use simple acts of social purpose to drive success and wellbeing. To listen to the entire interview, go to PerformanceDrivenThinking. com/Giving or scan the QR code to visit the page.

We also recommend connecting with Bea on social media:

LinkedIn: https://www.linkedin.com/in/beaboccalandro
Twitter: https://twitter.com/Beaboccalandro

CHAPTER 7

How to Lead Giving Teams

No people were ever honored for what they received.
Honor has been the reward for what they gave.
—Calvin Coolidge

Have you ever seen a gravity well? If you have been to a science center or other public space where curiosity or physics are explored, you probably have. A gravity well looks like a giant flattened funnel. On one side, you can drop a coin and then see it go round and round the top of the funnel, slowly making its way toward the center.

Then the coin eventually seems to move faster and faster as the centrifugal force pulls it downward and closer to the middle. Then the coin seems to spin faster, reaches the middle, and eventually drops into the collection bin underneath the gravity well.

There are two principles we can learn about giving from a gravity well. First, it makes giving a lot of fun. Who doesn't enjoy seeing a coin make its way around the funnel and then pick up speed before it drops with a dramatic clank into the bin? Kids of all ages enjoy this.

Second, it uses the principles of speed, force, and gravity to consolidate the coin along with many others. There is a great lesson here for anyone leading teams. Motion, speed, and gravity can work emotionally in your favor as you consolidate people's efforts to achieve something together you could never achieve on your own.

These principles lie at the heart of giving teams. In this chapter, we'll explore how these work and flesh out some practical tips for helping your teams become more giving. We'll start by investigating what prevents a giving culture, look at some core values of a giving culture, then share ten commandments to follow if you want to lead a giving team.

What Prevents a Giving Culture?

A great culture doesn't happen by accident. It must be intentionally developed over a period of time. Leaders sometimes work hard for years to develop a culture but are frustrated when it doesn't come together.

Here are a few reasons why your culture may be faltering a bit, or why people simply are not giving. Each of these reasons comes down to leadership. We don't want to pick on leaders, but leaders create a culture whether they realize it or not. That is one of the main functions of leadership.

Reason #1: Leaders only care about the bottom line.

You can try to project an atmosphere where people are valued, but ultimately, they know what is most important. You cannot conceal your true motives as a leader. It all comes down to what you feel the purpose of business is. Do you exist just to make a profit? Or do you exist for a higher purpose? Do you truly care about the welfare of your team?

Leaders who want to create a culture of giving will pour into their team members. It will look different from place to place, but you will see the value of developing people and giving them opportunities to grow and learn.

But if you only care about the bottom line, you will only see employees and team members as a means to a more important end. We would argue that people *are* the end. It's all about people.

Retail establishments are notorious for taking a bottom-line approach to culture and managing people. It is not unusual to hear about companies running through employees, especially around the holidays, because the culture is so bad in those places. When team members are not cared for, they have zero motivation to give.

Reason #2: Leaders are distracted by their problems.

Nobody is perfect, and everybody has problems. That's a simple fact of life. However, when those problems continue year after year and a leader is not emotionally able to deal with them, or is unwilling to deal with them, it affects the whole organization.

We know of one small nonprofit organization that had incredible potential. It was situated in a bustling suburban area in the Midwest. The staff was hardworking and motivated, and the organization had a successful track record of impacting the community.

However, the organization's director had serious emotional problems, which made them controlling, deceptive, and manipulative. Nearly the entire staff turned over in just four years, some positions having multiple people in that time period. This leader was unable to cope with the stress of the job because they were totally consumed by their own problems.

Distracted leaders are ineffective because they don't have the mental and emotional reserves to deal with the multitude of problems that any leader faces. Especially at a small organization, a leader typically wears many hats and deals with an array of problems and personalities on a daily basis.

Reason #3: Leaders don't emphasize giving.

Sometimes giving just gets lost in the shuffle of leadership. In reason #2 above, we talked about a distracted leader. One of the casualties of distraction is that nonessential functions get tossed aside in favor of more urgent matters, like production and payroll.

The vast majority of leaders believe in giving as a great principle to follow. However, it sometimes just gets lost in the day-to-day responsibilities of life. If a leader doesn't make giving a priority, it probably will not happen, simply because it's not a priority in their own mind.

Reason #4: Leaders don't deal with unresolved conflict.

We are familiar with a university where unresolved conflict nearly brought the whole institution to a collapse. In an unusual set of circumstances, several faculty members were engaged in conflict with one another and with the leadership, even to the extent that lawsuits were brought.

The university leadership was overwhelmed by the complexity and depth of the conflict, and although ultimately all those faculty members left (as well as numerous other administrators and staff), it left a deep lasting scar on the organization.

Interpersonal conflict is like a wound that is left open. It never has the chance to heal, and even if it does, it will leave a scar that never goes away. When people don't resolve their conflict, it forces others in their circle to take sides. Eventually, it creates even more conflict because it was allowed to fester and grow.

Why, then, do leaders let conflict go unresolved if it is so dangerous? The main reason is fear. They are afraid of confrontation, of making someone angry, of taking sides, or of wading into the murky depths of conflict resolution. They don't want to appear too soft or too harsh. Ultimately, they simply let it go for too long because they don't want to make the wrong decision.

In doing so, they create a much worse situation because all the while, the conflict grows and causes even more irreversible damage. It is impossible to establish a culture of giving and generosity in this kind of environment.

Reason #5: Leaders don't treat their people fairly.

We know that "fairly" is a loose term and can be interpreted many ways. After all, who determines what is fair? What seems fair to one person may not seem fair to another. (That is why we have conflict.) But that aside, most people have a good sense of what is fair and what is not.

The biggest area where fairness is concerned is compensation. If people don't receive regular evaluations and a consideration for a raise, they will not feel compelled to give. We know of one organization where the pay for part-time staff has not changed since the mid-1990s! And its leaders wonder why people do not feel compelled to give back to the organization.

If you aren't sure whether your team feels compensated fairly, just ask them. Leaders are afraid of what they will hear, so they often don't ask. But it's not just about the compensation for the work they are doing; it's also about the opportunity for advancement. If a team member has earned out and there is no chance of earning more, what motivation do they have for giving more to the organization?

John Ruhlin, author of *Giftology*, said, "You should never treat your employees in a mediocre way. It amazes me that budgets don't allow for $100 to spend on employee appreciation, yet we willingly blow through tens of thousands of dollars on trade shows and logo shirts." There is great value in treating your team members well and making them feel appreciated.

Core Values of a Giving Culture

Now that we have identified some of the obstacles that prevent us from developing a culture where giving is the norm, let's turn our attention to how to actually lead giving teams.

Before we offer specific strategies in the form of ten "commandments," let's briefly think through the core values of a giving culture. Values are the concepts and priorities that are most important to your culture at the end of the day. Here are nine core values we consider most important to developing a giving culture.

1. Abundance

Abundance means having more than enough or enough to go around. It is not so much concerned about what is there, but about how you perceive it. A person with a scarcity mentality can look at their surroundings, and all they see is a lack. A person with an abundance mentality can look at the exact same thing, and they see possibilities and growth.

Do you see possibilities everywhere? Do you assume the best is yet to come? Do you feel the best days are in front of you, not behind you? Do you see loads of new business out there, just waiting to be developed?

2. Stewardship

As we discussed in chapter 1, stewardship is the idea that everything belongs to God, and we are just managers of it. It's the sense of being a caretaker of someone else's property. How does your team perceive its resources? Do you see your building, assets, people, and other resources as belonging to God? Do they feel a responsibility to use those resources well?

3. People-first stance

A people-first stance can be hard to quantify, because profits are important. If you are not profitable, you won't be able to provide jobs for very long for the people in your care. Therefore, it is a balance. That being said, do the people on your team care for one another? Do they feel you are helping them develop to their full potential, as opposed to seeing them as mere cogs in the machine?

4. Future focus

If an organization has been around for some time, it is inevitable that people will think about its past. There may have been good and bad times, but you cannot stay stuck in the past. Are you willing to innovate? Are you willing to change with the times?

Many educational institutions are facing these questions now. They have done the same thing for generations, but they sometimes forget they are not in the degree-granting business—they are in the education business.

Education can take many different forms. No matter what industry you're in, you must be comfortable embracing change and being clear on what your business is.

5. Flexibility

You can always tell when a culture is inflexible because people focus on problems instead of possibilities. If you are stuck in doing the same things in the same way you have always done, you will see any deviation from that as a problem because it throws a wrench into your finely tuned system. However, with the rapid pace of change we are all dealing with in the modern age, change happens constantly. We must be flexible and nimble enough to not just navigate changes, but actually embrace them.

6. Ownership

This sounds like the opposite of stewardship, but it's just two sides of the same coin. Stewardship is all about taking care of someone else's property. Ownership is about taking personal responsibility for yourself. While every team member cannot own part of the company (unless they are shareholders), they are definitely owners in the sense of feeling responsible for the overall success of the organization.

How is the ownership culture in your neck of the woods? Do people shift responsibility and put blame on others? Or do they take personal responsibility for their shortcomings and ask how they can do better in the future?

7. Excellence

There is a lot of confusion about the meaning of excellence. Most people think of excellence as some unobtainable goal, something that is beyond their reach. But excellence is within everyone's reach. It simply means doing the best with what you have.

What resources, money, opportunities, talents and skills, people, facilities, relationships, and creative ideas do you have? Use those to the best of your ability and you will be pursuing excellence.

You cannot compare your best to someone else's best. Your biggest competitor is *you*. You are really competing only against yourself and your own potential.

8. Personal growth

A giving culture is by definition a growing culture. It is very difficult to give if you are not growing. Any sort of organizational or company growth must have personal growth as the foundation. Does your culture encourage personal growth? Do you give people opportunities for mental, physical, emotional, social, and intellectual growth? Do you give them resources and opportunities?

Here's an example: We heard of one college that carefully monitored the student evaluations of their professors, yet the college never set aside funds for faculty development. If teachers wanted to buy books, attend a conference, or grow in their development in ways that would directly benefit students, they had to pay for it themselves.

Many organizations do the same thing—they expect the best but do not invest in their people. Make sure you are giving your people the resources and ability to pursue personal growth and development.

9. Teamwork

It has been said that teamwork makes the dream work, and that is absolutely true. Earlier in the book, we mentioned the principle of synergy:

Two can accomplish more together than they can alone.

The same is true for any size team. Do the people on your team believe in teamwork? Do you have regular meetings to communicate, activities to build teamwork, and opportunities for people to work together? Giving is a team sport, and when people have their own silos and don't work together, they will be much less motivated to work together and give more.

One company that embodies all these values and more is Chick-fil-A. Founder S. Truett Cathy started with a vision that a "great company is a caring company." Chick-fil-A is known for its generosity and caring spirit within the communities they serve. For example, many Chick-fil-A operators sponsor national programs and local partnerships, support troops through appreciation events for the military, or hold fundraisers for local schools.

In addition, the Chick-fil-A Foundation aims to further Cathy's legacy of giving and goodwill by nourishing the potential in every child, particularly in the areas of education, homelessness, and hunger.

The company website lists the following initiatives:

- "To support education, the Foundation expanded its partnership with Junior Achievement USA, which offers kindergarten–12th grade programs that foster work-readiness, entrepreneurship and financial literacy skills to inspire nearly 5 million students each year to dream big and reach their potential."
- "To address youth homelessness, The Foundation is partnering with Covenant House International, which has helped transform and save the lives of more than a million homeless, runaway and trafficked young people—reaching 70,000 youth each year."
- "To fight hunger, the Foundation is partnering with Feeding America to donate to a local food bank for every new restaurant we open."

These are remarkable ways that Chick-fil-A gives back to the community and the world. However, none of it would be possible if not for the company culture of giving that was established from the very beginning. The simple "my pleasure" each customer hears from team members is a symbol of the deep culture of caring and generosity that permeates every level of the company.

To read more about Chick-fil-A's philosophy of giving and community involvements, visit https://www.chick-fil-a.com/about/giving-back.

The Ten Commandments of Creating a Giving Culture

Despite calling these the ten commandments, these are not words from God. Rather, they are words of experience based on our years of leading teams in a variety of settings.

Remember, you must be intentional about developing a giving culture. These suggestions will serve you well as you seek to develop teams of people who are giving and generous.

1. Thou shalt remember that culture can be created.

Perhaps you started your organization. Maybe the organization has been around a long time and you are the latest in a long line of leaders. You may be a leader in a new role, and things have been in decline for some time but you are doing everything you can to turn things around. No matter the situation, remember that you can turn your culture around.

You can set the example, speak into people's lives, and create a new pathway forward. It will not be easy, and it will take more time than you think. You will lose people along the way but also gain some new ones. Those are natural things that happen for any leader who is trying to establish a new culture.

2. Thou shalt keep thy pulse on the culture of your organization.

How do you do this? By keeping your ear close to the ground and paying attention to what is happening. So many leaders don't have any idea what is really happening within their organizations. They are surrounded by yes-people who are afraid to tell the truth.

One great way to keep your pulse on what's happening is simply by walking around and talking to people, and another is having an open-door policy. Both of these approaches involve keeping an open relationship with people at every level.

3. Thou shalt believe in the power of giving.

Do you personally believe in the power of giving? If you don't, it will eventually show. You can only put on a front for so long. We strongly encourage you to examine your heart and ask whether you are truly committed to giving not just as a business strategy, but as a lifestyle and a way of viewing reality.

If you personally believe in giving, your enthusiasm will show through. In fact, you will not be able to hide it! But if you are only giving because it seems prudent or because of the PR value, there will be a crack in the seams of your sincerity.

4. Thou shalt model the behavior you want to see in your team.

We don't just mean whether you are personally volunteering for causes your organization supports, or whether you are giving financially to other causes. In your interactions with team members at all levels, are you a giver? Are you a listener? Do you show empathy? Do you personally help people who need it? Do you compensate them fairly?

There are limits to this, of course, and no one has all the resources of the world at their disposal. But you must personally demonstrate the attitude and behavior you expect of your team. Otherwise, they won't follow your lead, no matter how much you talk about why it's important.

5. Thou shalt show your team how their giving makes a difference.

People want to see the results of their giving. You can do this in a bunch of ways, but the general rule is that putting a human face on giving makes a huge difference. People are ultimately interested in other people, and if you can show how their giving impacts other human beings, that goes a long way toward motivating them to continue giving.

6. Thou shalt give your team a variety of opportunities to give.

As we have mentioned before, people enjoy giving in a variety of ways. Some like volunteering, some like giving financially, some like working directly with people, some like organizing, and so on. Don't just offer one way to give and expect everyone to react with the same amount of enthusiasm.

Not every giving opportunity will excite people the same way. As you are thinking through ways your team can give, ask for help in coming up with creative ways people of different skill levels and personalities can get involved.

It is also important to think about how different generations like to connect with giving. Boomers, Gen Xers, Millennials, and Gen Zers all have different levels of trust in companies and traditional institutions. Younger generations want to be more socially involved but generally have less money. Older generations tend to have more money but are usually less technically inclined. So make sure to involve different generations in your decision-making process and ways to get involved.

7. Thou shalt make giving voluntary.

If you want to have your organization begin giving more, it will be tempting to create policies around this to normalize behavior. This may feel right because your motivation is correct.

But be careful about making giving a mandatory requirement. Each will be different. However, when people are forced to give, it's not really giving, is it? It is much better to lead by example and with an invitation to give rather than trying to motivate people by guilt or coercion.

8. Thou shalt remember people's number one emotional need: to feel affirmed and validated.

If people do not feel cared for or, at worst, if they feel taken advantage of, they will not be inclined to give. Yes, people work for money, but they also work out of a sense of purpose. They want more than just a paycheck.

This applies especially to younger generations, who want more from a job than their parents or grandparents wanted. They want meaning, purpose, and a chance to make a difference. They want to know that their work matters. When they feel validated and affirmed in their purpose and in their skills, they will open their hearts to giving.

9. Thou shalt make your organization a fun place to work.

On the surface, it would seem like certain workplaces and organizations would be more fun by definition. For example, you would assume a car repair shop would be less fun than a party supply store. But the industry or niche has nothing to do with the level of enjoyment people have in their job.

For example, we know a young man who works at a party supply store, and he is miserable. The management is terrible, the pay and the morale are low, and the whole affair is disorganized. On the other hand, we also know of a real estate company that goes above and beyond in creating a culture of fun and joy in their workplace.

You can do the same. If you don't project a sense of fun yourself, enlist the help of one or two team members who are great at celebrations and social gatherings. Put them in charge of fun within your team. People want more than just a paycheck from their jobs—they want meaning, relationships, and to enjoy their work.

10. Thou shalt always be creating culture.

Here's the good and bad news. The bad news is that culture can fall apart over time. Nothing lasts forever. As new team members arrive, and as others leave, the culture will change. If you are not intentional about keeping a giving culture alive, it will fade away. But the good news is that it's easy to sustain a great culture if you have already built one.

It takes a lot of work. When you incorporate team activities, great communication, and the help of those who are gifted in this area, you can sustain a great culture over time. They say that "vision leaks," but culture does, too.

We'll repeat what John Maxwell says about leadership: "Leadership is influence." Do you want to be comfortable in your role, or do you want to bring about positive change as a leader? If so, it will mean you must get uncomfortable and do what is needed rather than what only feels good. Yet this is the call of the leader: You are called to lead, which means going out front of the troops and forging a new pathway.

Is it frustrating sometimes? Yes. Do you often feel that you're inadequate? Yes. Will you get discouraged and wonder if you are making any difference? Yes. But the price of leadership is small compared to the influence you can have over years and decades of leading well.

When you do, you can multiply your impact infinitely as you develop people who not only influence their own areas and your organization, but thousands (or millions!) of others whom they influence.

Keys to Performance-Driven Giving

In order to lead giving teams effectively, consider the following:

1. Do you agree with our list of obstacles that prevent a giving culture? Do you sense any of these are present within your organization? If so, which of those did you inherit, and which do you feel you have contributed to?

2. Which of the core values do you personally relate to the most? Why? Write one paragraph describing why it's so important to you. Use that as the basis for team communication within the next weeks so your team can see your heart and what is important to you.

3. Review the ten commandments of creating a giving culture. Are you currently implementing any of these? It's easy to feel overwhelmed by all our suggestions, but remember that you are doing some things right. Choose one or two of them to focus on in the next quarter.

What if You're Not the Leader?

You may have read through this chapter and thought, *David and Bobby, all this sounds great, but I'm not the leader!* We understand that some people may feel frustrated by their inability to bring change to a culture that needs it, especially when they are not in charge.

If so, we hear you! That's why we have created this special section with a few reminders on how to be an influencer when you're not in charge.

You are more powerful than you realize.

Due to the advent of social media and an increasingly global culture, today anyone can have a huge impact. Remember that you can influence a large number of people with your words and actions. It doesn't matter if you're the leader. You can still communicate stories and content that change how people see the world.

Create a micro-culture around you.

You may not be the leader of the organization, but you have a sphere of influence. Maybe you're a department head or lead a small team. But even if you don't have any direct reports, you can still influence the culture around you.

How? Simply by being generous, thoughtful, and helpful to people around you. Influence goes in every direction, and you can create a micro-culture within your network.

Be a cheerleader for your organization and its leaders.

Cheerleading is a great use of social media and other creative tools such as blogs, podcasting, and video. If a picture is worth a thousand words, you can have an outsized impact by taking the initiative and being a major cheerleader and supporter of your organization.

As social media influencer and entrepreneur Gary Vaynerchuk says, "Document, don't create." When you document the positive things happening in your area and highlight people who are making a difference, people will notice. You might just create a new job for yourself!

Remember that positivity is contagious.

Negativity is contagious, but you can combat it with your positive attitude. We drift toward negativity because that is our human nature. We tend to notice the things that are wrong and focus on those.

But it doesn't have to be that way. With a positive attitude and a caring spirit, you can spread the love and begin to change a negative or uncaring culture.

A Conversation with Dan Cockerell, Former Vice President of the Magic Kingdom

This chapter has focused on how to create a giving culture within your company or organization. In this interview, we speak with Dan Cockerell, who literally wrote the book on how to create the right type of culture for your team.

Dan is the former vice president of the Magic Kingdom at Disney World. When he retired a few years ago, he was leading twelve thousand cast members, who entertained over twenty million guests annually.

That role was the culmination of a long and successful career at Disney, where Dan held various executive operations roles over the years, both in the theme parks and in the resort hotels. Now Dan is a speaker and coach who focuses on leadership and management practices that draw on his extensive career at Disney.

Dan is the author of *How's the Culture in Your Kingdom? Lessons from a Disney Leadership Journey.* The book is filled with lots of fun stories and examples of how to improve the culture in your personal and work life.

We spoke to Dan about his experience at Disney helping to create and maintain a great culture, and what every leader can learn from it. Even at the most magical place on earth, leaders still have to work hard to keep the focus where it needs to be.

We began our conversation with Dan by asking how he modeled the type of culture he wanted to create.

> *This was actually one of my favorite parts of the job. I was responsible and accountable for the twelve thousand people that worked at the Magic Kingdom Park, and I took it very seriously.*
>
> *I approached it a few different ways. The first was to be a role model for my direct reports. I had several general managers reporting to me who ran the different lines of business: food and beverage, merchandise, entertainment, operations, and engineering. The big thing I would do*

with them is to treat them the way I wanted them to treat their management. By role modeling, you set the tone for the organization.

When they came to me with a mistake and they were figuring out how to correct it, I was very much a helper. When I had high performers, I knew they were going to make mistakes. It was about problem solving.

They would use me as a model, and this would trickle down to the whole organization. People would see how we behaved and would understand what the culture needed to be like. This would work its way through the structure and hierarchy so that people felt comfortable telling their boss when things were wrong, or giving them critical feedback so we can get better.

We also wanted to discover what Dan had to say about creating a great culture by hiring the right type of people in the first place.

One of the big things people don't think about is that if you want people to fit into your culture, you should do your best to hire people who already have your values and are going to be a good fit.

People ask me sometimes, "How do you get so many people at Disney to be so nice and kind? How are they so service-oriented?" And I say, "Well, I'll tell you a secret. We stack the deck. We hire people who are already like that." A lot of organizations hire people thinking that they're going to change them, or they hire them not realizing how important it is to hire people who will be a good fit for the culture to begin with.

Let's take teamwork, for example. When I would interview people coming into Disney, one of the questions was, "How important is working independently to you?" That's not a trick question, and there is no wrong answer. But if someone said they do their best work independently, that would be a red flag. I knew they were probably not going to work well at Disney, because everything we did was interdependent. Everything was collaborative.

If someone answered that they loved working on team, we would ask for examples from their career or work life. If we could clearly see that they thrived in that environment, we knew they were going to be a good fit at Disney.

We wanted to find those employees who enjoyed service. If you like service, you will love hospitality. And that's what business Disney is in.

Disney has been known for its innovative and creative culture for decades. We were curious about the connection between these two sets of values: giving and generosity, and innovation and creativity. Here is Dan's response.

Yes, I absolutely believe there is a connection. We have been talking about collaboration. Collaboration is when you are generous with your ideas. You're generous with your support. When that happens, creativity and innovation happen.

We typically think of creativity as the result of a single brilliant moment, sort of the "light bulb" moment. But that's not the way it usually works. It usually happens when people are in their environment, interacting with others. Then they will interact with concepts and people outside their normal environment. They will take an idea from the other environment and then bring it into theirs.

Uber is a good example of this. Two guys come out of a bar, and one of them says, "I can't get a taxi. What if every car could be a taxi? How cool would that be?"

A lot of organizations have a competitive environment. People don't share ideas or concepts. They don't help each other. They are worried the other person is going to get ahead, so everyone holds back, and everyone suffers, and the organization doesn't get all the benefits of being creative. If people are willing to help each other, the company can get a lot better result.

This type of generosity in collaboration creates a culture of creativity. That's a beautiful thing.

Thanks, Dan! You are a shining example of a creative and collaborative leader, and we appreciate your words of wisdom.

Dan's website is https://dancockerell.com. Make sure to also check out his fantastic book, *How's the Culture in Your Kingdom?*, which will help you build the best culture possible where your people can thrive. To listen to the entire interview, go to PerformanceDrivenThinking.com/Giving or scan the QR code to visit the page.

We also recommend connecting with Dan on social media:

Facebook: https://www.facebook.com/dan.cockerell
LinkedIn: https://www.linkedin.com/in/dancockerell
Twitter: https://twitter.com/DanCockerell
Instagram: https://www.instagram.com/dancockerell
Podcast: https://dancockerell.com/come-rain-or-shine

CHAPTER 8

Dealing with Non-Givers

Only a life lived for others is a life worthwhile.
—Albert Einstein

One of the most important frameworks used in storytelling is the "hero's journey," popularized by the educator and author Joseph Campbell. The hero's journey describes the elements common to many cultures around the world over the last several thousand years as they have communicated their myths and stories. He popularized the hero's journey in his widely known book *The Hero with a Thousand Faces*.

One of the key elements of the hero's journey is the refusal of the call. This is the part of the story where we have already met the hero, there has been an inciting incident that set the story in motion, and someone is beckoning the hero on a grand adventure.

Perhaps you didn't realize it at the time, but you have seen the refusal of the call played out many times in popular stories and movies:

- *Star Wars: A New Hope*: Obi-Wan Kenobi invites Luke Skywalker to join the rebellion, but Luke has responsibilities on the family farm.

- *The Lord of the Rings: The Fellowship of the Ring*. The wizard Gandalf implores the Hobbit Frodo to join him on the quest to destroy the ring, but Frodo doesn't think he's capable.
- *The Wizard of Oz*: Glinda the Good Witch tells Dorothy Gale that the only way back home is by visiting the Wizard at the Emerald City, but Dorothy doesn't want to go.
- *Harry Potter and the Sorcerer's Stone*. Hagrid tells Harry Potter, "You're a wizard!" but Harry doesn't believe him.

When it comes to the journey of giving, some people will refuse the call. They don't want to take the journey with you. All the concepts we have discussed so far in the book will help you take yourself and your organization to the next level of giving, but if you don't deal with the non-givers, it will compromise your ability to give as much as you can.

In this chapter, we will look at why some people don't give, practical ways to handle non-givers, and how to help people without using money.

Why Don't People Give?

In chapter 4, we talked about indifference and how it is the biggest enemy of giving. Here in this chapter we will explore how to deal with people who are indifferent.

When they aren't giving, what can we do? How can we help them engage? Those are great questions, but we must first explore why people don't give in the first place. What causes indifference?

There are three primary obstacles: internal, external, and philosophical. When you are dealing with team members or others around you who are not giving, these can be real issues. It's also important to know that these may be real only in the mind of the person you're dealing with. Many times, we make up our own realities. We see pieces of information and create stories out of them. Perception equals reality.

Internal Obstacles

These are roadblocks inside the person's own mind. Whether perceived or real, these are realities they feel to be true. Let's focus on two main internal obstacles.

The first is a lack of faith. Faith is belief in something that is unseen. For example, if you are waiting for a taxi and believe it will arrive, you have faith in the taxi driver. If you don't have faith in the taxi driver, you will act accordingly and take another course of action, such as walking or calling a friend for help.

Likewise, when people are not acting how they should, it is often a lack of faith. Maybe they don't have a strong spiritual foundation and don't believe that God is involved in the giving process. They also may not have faith in your leadership or in the organization's mission. In addition, maybe they don't have faith in the causes or other organizations you are supporting.

In their mind, they may have perfectly good reasons for this. And it's also an ideal time to ask whether their lack of faith—particularly in your leadership or the organization—has any merit. For example, if you keep setting unrealistic expectations for sales or production, you have probably lost some of the faith of your team. So their skepticism may be grounded in reality.

The second internal obstacle is fear. If they are having issues at home or money problems, they probably are dealing with a lot of fear in their heart. When someone is struggling financially, it's scary. You don't know how things are going to turn out. You are driven by a fear of a catastrophe happening any moment. This fear can lead to distraction and a desire to protect what you already have at all costs instead of being open to giving.

External Obstacles

External obstacles are challenges or situations outside of the person. They have limited or no control over these. Although we can all choose how to deal with external problems, these obstacles are still a reality and must be dealt with or eliminated if the person can rise to their full potential as a giver.

This is a great time to examine whether they have opportunities to give in your organization. Sometimes we believe we are being clear and communicating well, when in fact our communication is muddy and unfocused. Make sure that you are not creating unnecessary barriers to giving. It's a situation where the emperor doesn't realize he has no clothes on!

Make sure you have a realistic understanding of what your team members are experiencing. In addition, maybe they have not been challenged to give. Sometimes the personal touch is all it takes to help someone feel engaged.

They may also be dealing with a difficult situation at home. Perhaps their spouse is not supportive of them giving their time, money, or other resources to help others. That is something you cannot control. The team member themself has limited control over this as well.

Philosophical Obstacles

These obstacles come down to the worldview of the team member. How do they perceive the world? Is it mainly good or bad, friendly or unfriendly? What do they believe about human nature, goodness, love, duty, and so many other big-picture matters?

Do they believe in the value of giving? Do they believe in supporting humanitarian causes? Do they see the value in generosity? Do they believe the actions have consequences? Do they even value other people?

Some people don't believe in giving to the community because they view it as a form of punishment. Our legal system is set up to assign community service to offenders, whether it's juveniles, actors, or even famous individuals who get caught in college admissions scandals.

We have lost the knack for serving our community out of choice. It almost comes across as it if is being forced by the system. But serving your community is a privilege and honor. It is a passage to character and citizenship.

These are vital questions and issues you can explore in team settings, your communication, or with the person one on one. But never underestimate the power of philosophy, because our beliefs about the ultimate nature of reality drive everything we do.

How to Handle Non-Givers

Now that we have established some obstacles to giving, how do you deal with them? How can you help a non-giver more fully engage in the wonderful world of giving? We offer a few practical strategies in this section, but first, let's consider what it means to be a non-giver.

Truth be told, we don't really like the term "non-giver" because it implies that the person is not giving in any way. That is simply not true. Every person gives in their own way—or at least, they believe they are giving. Everyone probably sees themselves as kind, loving, generous, and many other things we ascribe to good people. But the actual results of what they are doing can be radically different.

So keep in mind that you may see an entirely different picture of the non-giver than they have of themself. It's also important to remember that everyone justifies their own behavior. Whatever we do, it is rationalized in our own minds. So do not assume that the non-givers' view of themselves is the same as how you see them.

With all that said, here are a few keys for dealing with people who are not giving in the ways we would like.

Culture

Whenever you are dealing with a problem, it's important to see whether you are contributing to it. Is there a possibility you are enabling the negative behavior through your own actions or your failure to establish the right type of organizational culture? Have you modeled the behavior you wish to see? Have you communicated your expectations and set a model of giving and generosity?

Whether it's a family, church, community, or business environment, every leader believes they are setting a good example and communicating well. But if you ask the people around them, it's often not true. So do a gut check and make sure you are modeling and communicating the type of culture that enables people to be joyful givers.

This is why it's important to have honest feedback. Many leaders cannot handle honest feedback because they don't want to know the truth. Or as Jack Nicholson says in *A Few Good Men*, "You can't handle the truth!"

Can you handle the truth? Whether it's through informal conversations or some kind of assessment or feedback instrument, make sure you have an accurate perspective on whether you are helping set the right type of culture.

Conversation

Once you have done an honest self-assessment, it's time to have a conversation with the team member who is not giving. This seems like such a simple thing, but it's shocking how many people don't have a face-to-face conversation as their first option when dealing with a problem. They will avoid it, talk around it, and try other indirect means of dealing with the issue instead of facing it head-on.

We do this because we don't like confrontation. And who does? Very few people want to put themselves in a circumstance where they are uncomfortable, or the other person will be uncomfortable. However, it is necessary in order to have clear communication and deal with the issue directly.

When you speak to the person, be direct and empathetic. People are used to their leaders not being concerned about their needs, so they will avoid having an honest conversation because they don't think the leader cares. However, you can be different and show that you care by confronting the issue head-on.

Find out why they are not engaged and giving. Perhaps they are having a hard time at home. Perhaps they are going through some health problems. Maybe there are some other issues happening that you aren't aware of. This is the essence of setting a good culture and being an effective leader—you care about your people and genuinely want to see how you can help.

It's also important to make sure and communicate that you are primarily concerned about them first, not what they can do for your organization or company. Most workers are not engaged, and they think the organization mostly cares about the bottom line. But if you can connect to their heart and discover what is going on, that goes a long way toward fixing the problem.

Challenge

Performance-driven people are not engaged in a culture where there are low expectations. And how could they be? They perform best when they are flying with eagles and soaring to new heights. It may be that all they need is a great challenge. Have you challenged your team member? Have you asked for their best? Have you put their talents and skills to good use?

You may need to show them how giving can make them a better performer. Remember, people are motivated by different things. Some are motivated by performance, some by altruism, some by relationships, some by money, some by achievements, and so on. Find out what motivates the person and then help them get engaged. Give them a project or assignment that will use their skills and get them motivated by doing what they do best.

You can also personally ask for their help. Most people love to help. While they may not always respond to a general plea or a volunteer opportunity, if you ask someone personally, they may be more inclined to help.

It all comes down to the fact that people want to feel valued, affirmed, and useful. If they feel they're making a real contribution, that is a great motivator.

Connection

Giving is ultimately a relational exercise. We can give alone, but it is so much more effective when it is part of a team effort, especially in an organizational environment where so much of our success comes from being part of a team. Is your team member connected with the larger group? How do they relate to others around them? Do they have good relationships?

Even introverts can thrive in a team-based situation, as long as they have enough time to themselves and time to work alone and reflect. Make sure the team member is connected with others who can help them be successful.

A lot of factors tat go into connection, but two critical ones are your physical space layout and your organizational structure. If you can find ways to help people feel connected and not isolated, that will help them stay engaged. Then they will be more likely to give.

In this chapter, we have tackled the difficult topic of how to handle non-givers. It's not a topic we love to talk about, but yet it's a reality of life when you are leading an organization, a family, or first and foremost, yourself. But rather than looking at it like a burden, we encourage you to approach it as an opportunity to help others grow and develop into their full potential as givers.

Keys to Performance-Driven Giving

In order to deal with non-givers in an appropriate way consider the following:

1. Do you agree with the reasons we presented that people do not give? Why or why not? Do you spot any of those reason within yourself at times?

2. Think about current or past co-workers. Would you categorize any of them as non-givers? If so, how did leaders deal with them? What did you learn from that experience?

3. Review the thirteen ways to give without using money from chapter 6. Which of those can you begin to incorporate into your own giving? Which of those can you encourage your friends, colleagues, or team members to do?

When the Non-Giver Is the Leader

This chapter would not be complete without addressing an obvious yet disturbing reality of leadership: Sometimes the biggest non-giver in the organization is the leader. Whether the leader is self-aware about their giving deficiency or not, their attitude and approach have a harmful impact on the culture of the whole team and its ability to give.

But what can you do? What approach should you take as a team member in this situation? Here are ten suggestions.

1. Don't assume you know everything that is happening.

It may be tempting to pin blame on the leader or point fingers. Even if you think you know the whole story, you may not. Employees and team members often think they have a good read on a situation, when in fact they might only have a partial picture of what is happening.

It is important to have some humility and understand that you probably only know part of the truth. The leader may be giving in ways that you don't realize.

2. Give and serve outside your organization.

Although it's important to keep giving to support your company or organization, you can also find other avenues. You are not limited to giving only to the place where you serve. If you have limited opportunities there, look for other organizations and opportunities where you can use your time, talent, and resources to bless others.

3. Find and emphasize the good things about the leader.

No leader is perfect—not by a long shot. But surely there are some good or admirable qualities of your organization's leader (unless you work in the mafia or a criminal organization—which you probably don't!). Although you can't just ignore bad qualities or obvious flaws, you can certainly draw attention to the good things about the leader.

Perhaps they believe they are giving in ways that are not obvious to the whole team. Make it your goal to discover what those things are, and help support those positive qualities or initiatives.

4. Publicly support the organization.

If the leader is involved in conflict, or if there is a lot of drama at your workplace, it may be difficult to feel you can publicly support it. However, it is important to present a united front and to publicly emphasize the good things about where you serve. If you cannot publicly support your organization or your leader, it is probably time to find a new place to serve.

5. Be grateful for the opportunity to build your leadership skills.

Nobody likes adversity or situations where there is conflict. However, those are the greatest testing grounds for developing your skills as a leader. Use the example of your organization leader to consider how you can improve both now and in the future as a leader.

What are the qualities you would like to change? How would you do things differently in their shoes? What are they doing that is ineffective? What is working or not working? Those are great questions you can apply to yourself to help build your own skills.

6. Watch your own attitude.

When you are in a negative situation, it is very easy to let your attitude begin to slide. Other people around you are probably negative, so it's tempting to go along and start to say bad things about the organization or the leader.

But remember that it works both ways—both negative and positive attitudes can be contagious! You can have a positive influence on those around you even in the midst of a less-than-ideal circumstance.

7. Set an example for those around you.

Continuing on from the last point, remember that you have a responsibility to lead. You may not be the president of the organization or even have a fancy title. But according to leadership guru John Maxwell, "Leadership is influence." If that is true, it means you can lead without having a title.

If you are a giver and have a generous attitude, that means you approach all of life as an opportunity to give and serve. Make sure to set a positive example to your supervisors, your colleagues, and those serving under you.

8. Present opportunities for the leader to give.

This may sound obvious, but has the leader been given opportunities to give? If they are a bit toxic (or perhaps a lot toxic), they might have been repelling people for some time—in which case they have probably not had people around them who are givers.

This means you have a perfect opportunity to help them develop their giving muscles. We often feel like our bosses are unwilling or incapable of change, but that is not true. Perhaps you can be the one to help them develop their giving skills.

---

9. Give them the benefit of the doubt.

Leading an organization—even a small one—is a complex affair, and it's important to give them the benefit of the doubt and assume they want to help. You probably don't realize how difficult it is to balance a variety of demands and priorities unless you have been in their shoes yourself. Don't assume you know what they are thinking or dealing with.

10. Give to the leader.

This is perhaps the most important strategy of all when it comes to being a good influence in a bad situation. Ask yourself whether you have personally given to the leader. Have you offered to help? Have you been positive toward them? Have you been supportive? Have you asked what you can personally do to lighten their load?

If not, you still have some work to do. The vast majority of team members in an organization would rather complain and be passive than take action. It is everyone's responsibility to contribute and engage. Honestly explore what you can do to personally assist the leader.

A Conversation with Aaron Walker, Life and Business Coach

Throughout this chapter, we have focused on strategies for dealing with non-givers in your life and business. This can be a delicate area because it requires a masterful blend of empathy, understanding, leadership, and vision.

When we were brainstorming whom to interview for this chapter, Aaron Walker was the obvious choice. He is a leader who not only lives out these values—he also helps others to develop them as well through his Iron Sharpens Iron Mastermind, which now has well over a dozen groups with national and international members.

Aaron is the founder and president of View from the Top, as well as the author of *View from the Top*, a must-read book that will show you how to live with significance and success. In addition, Aaron is also the founder of the Mastermind Playbook, which is an incredible resource for starting, running, and scaling masterminds.

Aaron has established a culture of giving and generosity in his organization. We began this interview by asking Aaron how leaders can do the same thing within their spheres of influence.

I think that in order to establish any culture, you have to be a participant yourself. And when we did that here by individually modeling the behavior and by giving. You certainly can't have that type of culture without the person at the top and doing it.

So in order to establish a culture of giving in any company or organization, we have to do it through demonstration, through actions void of arrogance. We want to share and participate, and we want to encourage others to do it.

But we don't want to do it from an egotistical standpoint. We want to do it with great humility. In order to establish a culture of giving, you must practice it from the top down.

We know that many reading this book are solo entrepreneurs or small business owners, so we asked Aaron how these leaders can begin giving in a way that makes sense for their organization.

Here's the thing. We have to develop a heart to give. Most people say, "When I get a lot of money, then I'll give." But it's not true. Money magnifies what is already in your heart.

If you are not giving now, I'm not saying you couldn't learn to do it in the future, but it would be difficult. We have to start out very small and discipline ourselves in order to give.

It's a real blessing to be able to give. I just want to encourage the people that are not givers. You can learn this trait. You have to be open. You have to be willing. You have to want to help others. I can't impose that on you. So what I would simply do is to start out small and work your way up to the larger gifts.

And they will come because you'll find out that you can't outgive the giver, right? You just can't do it. So for the employees, for the people that are around you, start small and you'll see what a blessing it is. And I promise you that it will be a blessing to the recipient as well.

I would also say this: In any organization, as well as in your family, I think the real key is to be a servant leader. And in order to be a servant leader, you have to be a giver. You are a steward over everything you have, whether that's your time, your talents, your money, and anything else.

If you do a great job in all of those areas in your life, it will come back to you exponentially.

But what if you are working for an organization where the leader is not giving? Maybe it's even a toxic culture. How do you give or be generous in that environment? Aaron had some words of wisdom for people who find themselves in that type of situation.

If you are doing this in an environment where the leader or the boss is not a person who gives, model it personally.

I'll give you an example. On a recent Black Friday, I took all my grandchildren to a Waffle House. We go to the same Waffle House every Black Friday. We pay for everyone's meal at the restaurant. It's just something we do.

Of course, we do this privately so the people around us don't know it. My granddaughter noticed there was a gentleman up at the register paying. She said, "Big A, there's a guy up there paying. I don't understand."

So I got up quietly, walked over to him and said, "Hey, we've got you." He said, "No, no, please let me do this." And I said, "No, we've got you." And he said, "You've already bought mine. I'm buying somebody else's."

And I started laughing and said, "It's contagious!" And it really is contagious. When other people around you see your acts of generosity, when they see you doing it very humbly, it's contagious.

I would just simply say to people that are in an organization, model it with humility. It will encourage people to do it, not in a way to bring light to yourself, but just to encourage others through acts of demonstration.

Thanks, Aaron! You are an amazing example of generosity, and we appreciate your words of wisdom.

Aaron's website is https://www.viewfromthetop.com. Make sure to also check out his amazing book, *View from the Top*, which will help you do more, become more, and live your life in a way that matters. To listen to the entire interview, go to PerformanceDrivenThinking.com/Giving or scan the QR code to visit the page.

We also recommend connecting with Aaron on social media:

Facebook: https://www.facebook.com/AaronWalkerViewFromTheTop
LinkedIn: https://www.linkedin.com/in/aaronwalkerviewfromthetop
Twitter: https://twitter.com/VFTCoach
Instagram: https://www.instagram.com/isi_mastermind
YouTube: https://www.youtube.com/channel/UCDkwb8Lma3iylfjjBDzsB2A

PART 3
Bearing Fruit

CHAPTER 9

The Power of Starting Small

If you can't feed a hundred people, then feed just one.
—Mother Teresa

Imagine you are standing at the top of a high mountain. You look around, breathe in the cold, fresh air and prepare for an experiment. You bend down and scoop up a handful of fresh snow, packing it into a ball. Then you walk to the edge, lay down the snowball, and let gravity take over.

You know what happens next. As the snow begins rolling down the side of the mountain, it picks up velocity and mass. In just a matter of a few seconds, it becomes twice as large, five times as large, ten times as large. It's growing exponentially as it continues down the mountain.

By the time it reaches the bottom and crashes with a loud thud, it is large as a house. What started off as a small, harmless ball of fluffy white snow became a powerful force that could move almost anything in its way.

As we move into the third part of this book, it's helpful to keep that picture in mind. We have suggested many ways to make a difference in your giving, but it does require starting. This is the part where so many people get hung up: They just don't start.

In this section of the book, we want to help you see how to branch out in your giving. We want you to see how small habits and making simple decisions about giving can radically impact your life and the lives of those you touch through giving.

In our previous book, *Performance-Driven Thinking*, we said this:

> So sometimes the problem isn't a lack of accomplishment. The problem may be a culture that does not recognize performance outside of total victory. This "all or nothing" thinking undermines the concept of Performance-Driven Thinking. Individual and professional goals were not set for overnight success. Goal setting takes a sustained attitude of performance.
>
> The idea of "one and done" performance, in most instances, is unlikely and unsustainable, and many times leads to mental and emotional defeat. It becomes too easy to give up Performance-Driven Thinking when we do not instantly receive the big trophy. The idea of small wins in reality means that any growth in our personal or professional performance is really a victory. We can sustain our Performance-Driven Thinking when we embrace those small victories and count them as wins.

When you are starting a new endeavor, it is easy to feel overwhelmed or discouraged. You won't do everything correctly. But we want to remind you that it's not an all-or-nothing proposition. You won't have overnight success. You need to have sustained giving over a period of time to make a radical difference. We don't want you to become defeated by having unrealistic expectations.

Any growth you experience will be a victory! That's why in this chapter, we want to help you think about the power of starting small. If you're a go-getter and love to make quick progress, this may feel like we are putting a regulator on your "giving gas pedal."

But that's not our intention at all. If fact, we want to make great progress! In order to do that, most people need to start a new habit in a small way that helps them make steady progress (more on that in the next chapter).

Remember that everything successful once started as something small. You don't need to a radical shift in order to be successful with giving. In this chapter, you'll see the advantages of starting small, why we often give up, and specific strategies for starting small in different areas of your life.

The Advantages of Starting Small

You are already familiar with the benefits of starting small. We all have skills that have been developed over time. It may be skills we use at work, or skills we use at home or as a hobby. No matter, everyone is good at many things, and each of those talents and skills were developed by starting small. Let's look at some examples:

Example #1: Learning an instrument. Do you play an instrument? If not, perhaps one of your kids does, or another family member. To achieve any sort of expertise as a musician, you must practice and play for at least several years. If you play guitar, you begin by learning how to hold the instrument, the names of the strings, and how to play a few chords.

It feels like you are making slow progress at first. Your fingers hurt, you struggle to play barre chords, and perhaps some of the strum patterns don't come easily. However, with time, you begin to get the hang of it.

Example #2: Losing weight. If you have ever been on a diet or weight-loss plan, you already know the importance of starting small. It is rare for anyone to jump into any kind of health-related goal, make massive changes to their diet and exercise, and stick with it.

This is why so many people join a gym at the beginning of the year, then cancel it just a few weeks later. Those who are successful over the long haul start out by making small changes to their diet and exercise and sticking with them over time.

Example #3: Earning compound interest. Many financial teachers and advisors have pointed out the magic of compound interest. If you have a $2,000 investment and it earns 10 percent, you will have $2,200 at the end of the first year. If you add just $200 to your investment each year, by the end of the second year you will have $2,620. It won't feel like you are making much progress. However, if you add $200 each year and continue to earn a 10 percent return, you will have $7,903 by the end of the tenth year. By the end of year 50, you will have $446,220! That's over two hundred times your initial investment plus a little extra each year.

You can clearly see that there are advantages to starting small and staying consistent. The value of your investment grows exponentially over time, whether that investment is money, diet and exercise, or practice time.

Let's look at a few reasons why starting small is such an advantage, as opposed to starting big.

You mitigate your risk.

Obviously, we are advocating that giving is a good thing. We are very much in favor of it! But we are also talking about giving from the other side, having been involved in giving for many years, in many different ways.

That is not necessarily other people's experience. It may not even be your experience. When you embark on a new habit or process, you don't know if it is going to work. It is important to start out small, because you minimize the risk and decrease the possibility of something going wrong.

When it comes to giving, it's not so much that something will go wrong, though. It's more a matter of you having the benefit of knowing that you only making a small change instead of jumping into something wholesale.

You get to see the process working.

If you are skeptical about giving, starting small allows you to see the process working right in front of your eyes. You don't have to take our word for it—you simply have to participate in the process and then witness the change that happens as a result.

Let's go back to the compound interest analogy we mentioned earlier. If you have ever invested, you probably looked at your quarterly investment statements or checked your account online. Although there are ups and downs in the market, overall you probably noticed that your account gets a little bit larger (on average) year after year. That definitely motivates you to keep on investing so you can see the results.

It is easier to get other people on board.

When you start anything new, it will likely not involve only you. It will also involve others, such as your family or your team at work. The beauty of starting small is that others can also see the process working and have time to emotionally adjust.

People process change at different rates. Some people embrace change quickly and love the challenge and excitement of a new adventure. Other people resist change even when there is a clear advantage to going along with it.

The majority of people take a wait-and-see approach. They are not necessarily eager to jump on board with a change, but they will do so when there are clearly defined benefits.

In other words, people adopt change when the pain of saying the same is greater than the pain of change. We naturally resist any kind of pain. So starting small is a great way for people dip their toe into the waters of giving to see how it feels before making a bigger commitment.

Taken together, all of these factors mean that over the long haul, you will be more likely to embrace the change and incorporate it into your life. That is exactly what we want! We don't advocate making a massive change in your giving right away, because you will probably not stick with it long-term.

Strategies for Starting Small

We want to emphasize that you don't necessarily need to make big changes in order to make a big impact. As we have seen, small changes, increased over time, can have an enormous influence. Let's dive into five areas where you can use the power of starting small.

1. Personal Life

Look for small opportunities to begin giving every day. If money is a concern, then don't begin, there since it's often a stress point with people. Sit down and make a list of five different spheres where you could begin giving each day. These might include your family, company, church, community, online friends or communities, students, colleagues, and other groups of people.

Now think about different needs each of those groups have. We'll talk about family in just a moment, so let's focus on people not in your family or work. Let's say you're a part of entrepreneur community online. What do those people need? That's right, they need promotion, referrals, and marketing. How can you take a few minutes each day to help promote their business or make connections?

That's just one example. Another example is to simply begin your day with a positive, giving attitude. If you journal, you can write something along the lines of "Today I choose to be grateful for life and to be a positive, giving person." Just that affirmation alone, written with your own hand, has a powerful mental effect.

If you don't journal, you can also record yourself saying something similar, or even look at yourself in the mirror while repeating it. These are just a few ideas, but you get the picture. There are all kinds of opportunities around you on a daily basis for giving if you will simply approach life in the correct spirit and choose to see with the eyes of a giver.

2. Marriage

Marriage is perhaps the hardest arena to start any kind of change. Why? Because our spouses know us intimately. They see us at our best and worst. They know the times when have made promises but did not keep them. So when we say we want to commit to something new, perhaps a new habit or program, they probably feel justified in being skeptical.

A great place to start is by simply having an honest conversation with your spouse. Why are you excited about giving? Where is their heart in relationship to giving? Where might they like to give? What can you work on together that would be meaningful? Those types of questions can be helpful in getting a conversation going.

If you don't currently work from a household budget, this is a small way to begin getting a better handle on your money. If you can start using a budget (and do it without killing each other!), then you can easily move the conversation into giving.

This is also a great time to ask how you are giving to your spouse. Are you emotionally available? Are you kind and thoughtful? Is your attitude right? If you are constantly irritable or lack thoughtfulness, it will be hard for your spouse to take giving seriously. They will wonder why you are so excited about being generous to strangers when you don't show the same impulse for giving in your own home.

3. Parenting

What we just said about giving to your spouse also applies when starting small with your kids. How do you relate with your children? Are you generous and kind? Do they know you as a kind and thoughtful person in your everyday interactions at home?

Kids don't require much to feel loved and appreciated. You can start small by having a weekly "date" with each of your kids, where you spend dedicated time with them. We recommend learning your kids' love language to see how you can best express your love and kindness to them.

Are you modeling giving behavior in your everyday life? Do your kids see you giving to your spouse? Kids learn best not by listening to a lecture, but by watching us. If they see you being generous and kind every day, they will be much more open to the idea of giving in their lives as well.

That's not to say you should not have direct conversations about giving, because you should. But they will be far more effective if those conversations are preceded by living out your giving.

4. Your Business or Organization (as a Leader)

You will see a pattern in this section: Some of what we said about marriage and parenting applies in the office as well. The main thing is to model giving behavior. As a leader, you are probably eager to start implementing practices or programs for giving in your organization. But remember that those will not be very effective if your team does not know you as a giving person overall.

Here's a great place to get started in a small way: Gather together a group of team members and ask if people feel you are a giving and generous leader. Now, you have to do this in the right way and with the right group. You need to have a high level of trust in your people. But when you do, their answers might surprise you.

Does your team feel as if they are treated fairly? Do they have regular evaluations or assessments? Are they compensated fairly? Do you have fair policies regarding time off, vacation, and related human resources issues? If they don't feel they are being treated fairly, any official giving program will ring completely hollow. They will resent it because they will wonder why you are giving to strangers when you don't even take care of your own team.

Giving can easily backfire in a climate where your team is frustrated at your lack of giving (or, we should say, a perceived lack of giving). They may think you are only giving for the PR value, which of course is not the main reason you should do it.

Assuming all those elements are good, we encourage you to start small. When Morgan James began a partnership with Habitat for Humanity, we did not have any money to give. But we called Habitat and told them we wanted to raise awareness for their cause, and then donate money as we earned more in our company. They were of course eager to accept that.

You can give as funds come in. Remember, you don't have to commit a certain percentage. Raising awareness of a cause or giving opportunity is the best place to start. Awareness will increase your partnership as well as your desire to give even more.

5. Your Business or Organization (as a Team Member)

But what if you are not the leader? What if you are not the one calling the shots? Good news: You can absolutely make a difference in your organization no matter what your role or position.

Start where you are, and start small. Is there any extra project that needs done in your area? Who needs help? Who needs a little encouragement? Those are great places to start. All it takes it just being aware of the needs around you.

You can also suggest opportunities for giving to your leaders. Maybe they are looking for a place to start giving but don't know where. Leaders always have a full plate, so if you can help identify potential giving partners or other information that would lighten their load, they will appreciate that. You can also give them this book!

If you were the supervisor, what kind of team member would you like to have? That is the key to being the type of team member who can help you leader give. But start small, first within your area, then as opportunities arise, present those to your leaders.

In his landmark book *The 7 Habits of Highly Effective People*, Stephen Covey wrote, "Sow a thought, reap an action; sow an action, reap a habit; sow a habit, reap a character; sow a character, reap a destiny." This is an apt way to summarize what we have tried to get across in this chapter. When you begin with correct thinking, it works its way all through your existence, eventually determining your destiny.

Every destiny begins with thinking and small actions. Take these small steps today to begin changing not only your own destiny, but that of so many others, including your family, workplace, and community.

Keys to Performance-Driven Giving

In order to use the power of starting small in building your giving habit, consider the following:

1. How much thought have you given to starting small when it comes to developing a new habit? How many of the advantages we listed do you relate to?

2. When is the last time you tried to establish a new habit but felt frustrated and gave up? Review the list of reasons that people give up when starting something new. If you relate to any of these, list the reasons why and how you can avoid it when starting small with giving.

3. Choose one of the life areas we listed for starting small (personal life, marriage, parenting, leading at work, and being team member at work). What is one small thing you could do in one of those areas in the next twenty-four hours?

Qualities of Small Starters

When you want to start small, what sort of qualities should you develop within yourself, and what should you look for in others? Here are ten qualities of people who start small and continue to develop their giving.

1. **Tenacity.** Do you persevere through challenges or give up at the slightest sign of trouble?
2. **Positivity.** Do you start each day believing the best about yourself and others, and do you share that outlook with others?
3. **Faith.** Do you believe God wants the best for you, and do you believe you are capable of greater things?
4. **Openness to change.** Are you willing to change in order to bring more blessings and abundance into your life?
5. **Valuing people.** Do you have a heart for people and an empathy for helping add value to them?
6. **Stewardship.** Do you see yourself as a steward of the blessings God has given you?
7. **Servant-mindedness.** Do you take joy in serving others, your family, and your organization?
8. **Big-picture thinking.** Do you see small starts as a way to get better over time, and can you see the bigger picture that is possible through starting small?
9. **Realism.** Are you prepared for the setbacks, discouragement, and problems that will always come when you try something new?
10. **Grounding in community.** Do you feel convinced that you are better when you are serving and giving in community with others?

A Conversation with John David Mann, *New York Times* Bestselling Author and Entrepreneur

You've just read about strategies for starting small. We can't think of a better way to conclude this chapter than by featuring a conversation with John David Mann. As the co-author of the international bestseller *The Slight Edge* (with Jeff Olson), he knows a thing or two about the power of starting small and developing great habits.

John also coauthored the international bestselling classic *The Go-Giver* (with Bob Burg), the *New York Times* bestsellers *The Latte Factor* (with David Bach) and *The Red Circle* (with Brandon Webb), as well as numerous other books. He has also written for *American Executive*, CNBC, the *Financial Times*, Forbes.com, *Huffington Post*, *Wired*, and many other outlets.

We began our conversation by looking at some ways that anyone can start giving in small ways.

> *The best place to begin giving is to start with the people around you in everyday life. Naturally, this means starting at home—your husband or wife, children, parent, brothers or sisters, and so forth. Then it extends to your friends, colleagues, and neighbors. We can start giving by finding little ways to invest in those relationships.*
>
> *That can be as simple as spending a few minutes listening. There is a tremendous deficiency of listening in our culture. It's made much worse by social media because there are so many more avenues for talking rather than listening. Go the extra mile and be a person who listens to others. It's one of the best ways to be kind.*
>
> *Another principle is giving the other person the benefit of the doubt. When you have the opportunity to be annoyed at something, choose the path of not being annoyed at all. Just say to yourself, "They probably have a very good reason for being cranky right now."*
>
> *There is a common misconception that we must get out of our*

comfort zone in order to grow. I don't agree with that. We grow by stretching the boundaries of that zone. If you jump out of your comfort zone and do something that makes you uncomfortable, it's easy to freeze. If you stay where you're comfortable and push a little, stretch a little, it's much easier to perform at your best.

John is known as a storyteller, and we were curious about the connection between generosity and storytelling. Here is his response.

In The Go-Giver, *Bob Burg and I focused on one overriding principle: taking the focus off yourself and putting it on the other person. It's not self-abasement; it's not martyrdom. It's simply a shift of focus. That really is true for being a storyteller.*

In order to tell stories well, you must shift your focus from yourself to your listener, audience, or reader. That's whom the story is for. Is storytelling fun? Of course! But ultimately, it's something you do for other people.

What do they want? What do they need? Who are they? Those questions can help you generously focus on others as a storyteller.

Speaking of *The Go-Giver*, we asked John about the final "Law of Stratospheric Success" found in the book: "Stay open to receiving." Why is it so difficult for people to learn how to receive?

Somehow we've developed this cultural message which says it's better give than receive, and that getting paid is dirty. There is a common perception that it's less noble to be the one receiving, and it's more noble to be the generous giver.

There is no doubt about the nobility of being generous. But guess what? Being a generous receiver is a good thing, too. It's hard for people to wrap their heads around that, because we are taught from an early age that it's better to give than receive.

If someone comes up to me and says they loved one of my books, it might be tempting to deflect the compliment and downplay the value of the book. That's what many authors do, because they can't receive a compliment well.

Why do we do this? Because the mythos of the underdog is so ingrained in our heads. Everyone loves an underdog. Everyone hates a tycoon. We love to see the powerful fall. There is a cultural narrative that if someone is accomplished or wealthy, they must have cheated to get there.

We like to avoid being that person and therefore reject blessings other people want to give us, whether it's a compliment or getting paid. It's just cultural immaturity, and we haven't yet trained ourselves out of it.

Thank you, John! We appreciate your insights about starting small, storytelling, and the power of receiving.

You can visit John's website at https://johndavidmann.com. We encourage you to check out *The Go-Giver*, a book that has impacted countless people by helping them to understand the power of giving. To listen to the entire interview, go to PerformanceDrivenThinking.com/Giving or scan the QR code to visit the page.

We also recommend connecting with John on social media:

Facebook: https://www.facebook.com/johndavidmann
LinkedIn: https://www.linkedin.com/in/johndavidmann
Twitter: https://twitter.com/JohnDavidMann

CHAPTER 10

Building a Giving Habit

I have found that among its other benefits,
giving liberates the soul of the giver.
—Maya Angelou

People who work at an office have a certain routine they follow each day.
When the workday is finished, they get in a car or take public transportation, travel for a while, and then arrive at a place they call home.

There are other words we use for this location, including "dwelling,"
"house," "pad," or even "crib." It is the place where we feel most comfortable, where we feel most welcome. It is our base of operation, the place
where we naturally return to again and again.

In the world of animals, this is called a habitat. It's the natural environment where a creature lives. The word "habitat" is closely related to
the word "habit." A habit is an action or activity so ingrained in our
behavior that we do it without thinking. You might say that a habitat
is the place where we dwell, whereas a habit is an action that dwells
within us.

In the previous chapter, we looked at the power of starting small.
When you start small, you have the power and the possibility of accom-

plishing big things. But how do you turn those small starts into long-term habits? In this chapter, we'll look at the roadblocks to a giving habit, strategies for developing it, and the results that come when you make giving a habit.

Roadblocks to Developing a Giving Habit

If it's important to develop a giving habit, especially when you take a "small wins" approach, as we talked about in the last chapter, what are the reasons we sometimes are not successful? And how can we navigate these roadblocks and let a giving habit take root when starting small? Here are a few roadblocks and how to deal with them.

You are trying to do it perfectly.

Perfectionists often have a hard time making positive changes. They have an internal switch that constantly cries out, "You must do it perfectly!" Perhaps they come from a family that always expected straight A's. Maybe the pressure comes from their own extreme expectations. No matter the source, the perfectionism is not healthy.

Only God is perfect. You will never be able to achieve perfection in your life. We can accept this intellectually, but it's hard to accept this emotionally if it is the way you have treated every new habit or goal in your life. Just know going into it that you will not be perfect, and that is okay. We are aiming for progress, not perfection.

You are too busy or distracted.

We live in an age of constant interruptions, media, distractions, and activity. If you are constantly switching your attention from one thing to the next, you will never have the time or emotional bandwidth to focus on a new habit.

If you want to make giving a true habit in your life, start small by taking just sixty seconds at the end of each day to evaluate your giving.

Think about the head, heart, hands framework we shared earlier in the book. How did you do in each of those areas?

Making progress doesn't have to take a lot of time. Just that one minute per day is a tiny step toward integrating better giving habits into your life.

You don't know where to give.

Maybe you want to give, but you don't know who or what should receive your giving. This is opposite of most people's approach. There are countless needs in the world around them, but they aren't willing to give. Either that, or they are simply blind to others' needs. Any way you slice it, you have a great problem: You are a giver who needs a receiver!

We will talk in detail later on in the book about choosing where to give. But for now, think about several areas where you can give: your church, nonprofits you know, or friends in need. And we don't mean just money, although that is certainly helpful. Think also in terms of giving your time, energy, and support.

You don't see your giving making a difference.

Maybe you have started to give, but you aren't seeing how it affects anyone. Let's say you have started to work with a local nonprofit who is a partner. You have started to promote their organization. Maybe some of your team members have even volunteered their time or you have donated funds or materials. But you aren't sure how your giving has actually helped them.

In a case like this, communication can eliminate a lot of misunderstandings. You can ask your contact at the organization (or their director) for information on how your giving has helped them. Or perhaps there is information on their website, or through other means, about how giving impacts people.

Remember that giving is not about you—it's about the other person. Sometimes when we start a giving habit, we want to see results right away. It's easy to become a little irritable or unhappy when it feels like we are doing good but don't see immediate results. But be patient, communicate with others, and trust that you are doing good in the world even if you can't always see the direct outcome.

You have opposition from your family or team members.

Opposition to your giving is a tough situation, especially if you don't like conflict. (And let's face it, most people do not like conflict.) If your vision for giving is different from that of those around you and you are not on the same page, it could spell trouble.

If this is the case in your situation, go back to good communication. Many problems can be worked through when you simply talk to the people involved. It's amazing how many people don't do this one simple thing! Find out why they are having an issue with giving and where the problem is. See if you can meet halfway or come up with a compromise or some way for both of you to be happy.

Sometimes when you have a conflict and honestly talk it through, you discover that you are the one who did not communicate well. When you are excited about a new project or direction, it feels great to dive into it headfirst. But the people around you have not had the benefit of going through the mental process that led to your enthusiasm. Help them see your reasoning and passion, and try to work it through to everyone's satisfaction.

You are in the middle of a crisis.

A final reason we sometimes fall off the wagon after starting a giving habit is that some kind of crisis happens. This is not under our control. Sometimes life just happens to us. Maybe it's an illness, job loss, family crisis, money problem, or other urgent situation.

In these moments, you either become bitter or better. We challenge you to find a way to continue giving so you can be a channel of blessing to others. What you will often find is that in the midst of a crisis, giving is a lifeline that helps you focus on other people's needs. Even when things are going badly in your life, there is always someone who has it worse. Giving helps you keep this vital perspective.

Now that we have dealt with some roadblocks, let's turn our attention to a few practical strategies for building a giving habit.

Keys to Building a Giving Habit

Building a great habit is not a one-size-fits-all approach. We are all unique based on our psychology, experiences, personality, and temperament. However, we offer this list knowing that no matter who you are, these principles will help you. We would also suggest reviewing our "Ten Steps to Sustain Performance-Driven Thinking" from chapter 10 of our previous book. That list makes a helpful companion to our suggestions here.

Start small.

In the previous chapter, we emphasized the importance of starting small. We mention it again here because many people want to dive into giving whole-hearted. Which is fantastic! But we would rather you make it a long-term habit than a big splash up front, yet you don't continue with it. Remember that big long-term habits are built on small, consistent actions over a period of time.

Recruit giving partners.

Giving is not a one-person show. You may be used to doing many things in life by yourself, perhaps even having lots of success. But when you partner with others, you can take advantage of the synergy that comes with partnerships. There are all kinds of ways to partner with others.

We suggest first of all partnering with your family, since they are your biggest allies and supporters (and you are likewise their biggest allies).

Your team at work, community partners, and those who receive your giving are all partners in the adventure of giving.

Make your giving automatic.

Technology today makes it very easy to automate your giving. You can set up auto-withdrawal using apps or tools that your bank makes available. Most likely, you have already automated some of your bill payments, so why not do the same with giving? Many times, we tend to make giving the last thing we do instead of the first.

We encourage you to make your giving the very first "bill" you pay each month. We know giving is not just about money. You can give in so many other ways. If you are volunteering or giving in nonmonetary ways, make it an appointment on your calendar, just as you would anything else.

Plan your giving.

Most people treat giving as something they do on impulse. If it is not something that is in their budget (whether financial budget or time budget), they only do it when they have the extra margin. And you can imagine how often people happen to have "extra" time or money—almost never!

People who want to be as generous as possible plan their giving. They don't wait until they have the impulse or the urge to give. Even though people who give randomly sometimes give a large gift, and it feels more exciting in the moment, those who plan their giving will typically give more in the long run. We want you to be performance-driven, which means you are giving because you want to become the best version of yourself. Planning your giving will absolutely help with that goal.

Another note: Planned giving is also much better for those receiving it. It is easier to manage a budget when you know what amounts will be coming in each month. Keep that in mind when deciding whether you will give sporadically or on a planned basis.

Consider multiple ways to give.

We have emphasized financial giving to a large degree in this book, but we want you to consider a broader, more holistic approach to giving as well. You can give through generous words, time with people, volunteering, gifts, and so many other ways. Don't neglect your skills when thinking about the most effective ways you can give.

Set giving goals.

We set goals for everything in life: Christmas savings, weight loss, training for a 5K race, work projects, writing deadlines, and so much more. But we often don't consider setting goals around your giving. But if giving is important to us, why wouldn't we set goals? When you are establishing a new habit, goals are a powerful motivator to keep going even when it feels hard.

When you set a giving goal, make sure it is reachable, but not too easy. We suggest setting a goal that is 20 percent beyond what you think you can reasonably reach. This stretch goal will make you a little uncomfortable, but it will still be in the realm of possibility if you give it a little extra effort.

An important tool in sticking with a habit and moving toward a giving goal is tracking. You can use a spreadsheet, app, or an old-fashioned pen and notebook to keep track of your progress. This way, you can see how far you have come and stay encouraged as you build this new habit.

Involve your kids or grandkids.

Kids love challenges, and no matter how old they are, they love to help with a family project. In addition to setting your own giving goals, get them involved in setting goals also. It doesn't have to be a money goal; it could be a goal to help others or to be kind. There are many ways to give and be generous.

When you involve kids, it motivates you, too, because it reminds you of the power of your own example. It's one thing to let yourself down; it's quite another to let your kids or grandkids down.

Celebrate small wins.

If you are a performance-driven person, you are likely more focused on achievement than anything else. Sometimes we high achievers don't stop to celebrate our accomplishments. When you reach a milestone, take some time to celebrate and reflect on what you have accomplished.

Even if you sometimes forget to celebrate or don't see celebration as important, others around you will see it differently. If you're not celebrating for you, then celebrate with others who feel a great sense of motivation when they celebrate.

Surround yourself with givers.

The concept of a mastermind has been around for a long time in the business and leadership world. A mastermind is a group of like-minded people who meet on a regular basis to help one another achieve their goals. The main idea is that you can accomplish more as a group than each of you can on your own.

As you embark in greater giving and establish stronger habits, make sure to surround yourself with like-minded givers. This probably means reducing the time you spend with non-givers. It also means increasing the time you spend with generous and thoughtful people. There are lots of ways to do this. You can ask people to lunch, interview them for a podcast, read their books, create a mastermind, have conversations, follow them on social media, and so much more.

The main point here is to be intentional about who you allow to influence your thinking. We have mentioned Earl Nightingale's famous quote before: "You become what you think about." When you surround yourself with generous people, you think about generosity more often.

Don't underestimate the power of influencers in your life, either for good or for bad.

Set reminders.

You don't need to stress out about remembering to give. You can automate the process by setting reminders. This can be a variety of tactics, including setting a reminder on your phone, putting an appointment on your calendar, or even hanging up a picture that reminds you to fulfill your commitment. When you combine this with other strategies we have mentioned, like involving your kids or setting goals, it's much easier to follow through on your intentions.

Practice habit stacking.

Habit stacking is the process of attaching a new habit to an existing one. You can stack them so the first one triggers the second one. Let's say you want to establish a habit of donating to a food pantry once a week. You can stack that habit on top of a weekly trip to the grocery store.

Another example would be giving to a church or other organization once a month when you pay your bills. If you are establishing a daily habit, you could use something like brushing your teeth as a trigger that sets the new habit in motion.

View life in terms of experiences, not things.

One of the big reasons that we get into trouble with a consumerist mentality is that we see our lives as a contest where the goal is to accumulate the most possessions. The winner is the one who has the biggest car, bank account, or house.

While it's wonderful to have nice things, the ultimate meaning in life is the relationships you develop with others and the experiences you have along the way. It's all about who you can serve and how you can give. Don't get caught up in the trap of becoming a consumer.

Be gracious to yourself.

When you are trying to get a habit established, you will fail. You will fall short and may even give up a time or two. We are often quick to extend grace to others but withhold it from ourselves. You aren't perfect—God is the only one who is perfect. When you mess up or fall off the giving wagon, just hop right back on and give yourself a little grace.

Remember why you are giving.

If you are task oriented, you can easily rush from one thing to the next, missing out on the whole purpose of giving. It's easier to stick with a habit if we keep the meaning at the forefront. Ultimately, we are honoring God and serving people when we give. It's not about checking a task off your list (although that may feel good, too).

Giving also helps you become a better leader and performer. We don't give in order to get, but the reality is that giving does help us grow stronger. It helps us become more successful and perform better in all areas of our lives. When you keep this perspective in mind, it's easier to keep going with a habit.

Keep an eternal perspective.

Above all, we must keep in mind that our giving will impact people long after we are gone. The momentary sacrifices we make during our life here on earth are tiny compared to the massive influence we can have in the immediate and distant future.

The Benefits of a Giving Habit

Now that you have established giving as a habit by using the power of small wins, it's time to enjoy the benefits of giving! Yes, it's true: Giving benefits more than just the recipient. It also benefits you by bringing many blessings into your life.

It's important to keep these blessings in mind when you're establishing a habit, because you may not see these benefits come right away. But trust us, they are right around the corner.

Giving becomes easier.

When you have established a giving habit, it becomes second nature, and you don't even have to think about it anymore. It has truly become part of you. At the beginning of this chapter we mentioned the connection between habit and habitat. When you establish a new habit, the action or activity makes its habitat inside you. You don't have to exert the same amount of effort to continue doing it, therefore making room for the next amazing habit you want to develop.

You attract more joy into your life.

This is an aspect of giving that is often ignored. We sometimes talk about giving as an act of duty or opportunity, but it's easy to forget about the pure joy that comes into your life as a result of giving to others. And who couldn't use more joy?

Your giving impacts other people.

We have mentioned this multiple times, but it's worth saying it again: Your giving impacts people. Whether you give to great organizations or direct your giving to individuals, those are human beings whose lives are changed because you gave. And that is worth celebrating! Not only that, but your giving impacts those who giving alongside you, such as your family, team members, or partners.

You increase your giving.

Giving is like exercise and health—the more effort you put into it, the more you *want* to keep doing it. When you establish a giving habit and then start to see how it changes both you and the people who receive your giving, you see more of those blessings in your life. You will also start to experiment by giving in different ways and seek out new opportunities.

You develop new and better habits.

We talked about habit stacking earlier in this chapter. As you develop your giving habit, you can then start to stack other new habits on top of your giving. Therefore, your personal performance and success becomes a never-ending loop that goes upward. Your habits build off one another and take you to even higher levels of impact and joy.

You won't always get it right. You will make mistakes along the way. You might even want to give up on your journey to making giving a habit in your life. However, remember to be a progressionist, not a perfectionist. The important thing is making progress over time. That's why we recommend starting with small wins.

Anne Morrow Lindbergh was the wife of Charles Lindbergh, who piloted the first transatlantic flight. Talk about an achievement! She saw firsthand how the power of small wins could help you achieve big goals over time. Anne famously said, "To give without any reward, or any notice, has a special quality of its own." We hope this chapter will help you make giving a habit so you can begin to experience the incredible feeling that giving can bring into your life.

Keys to Performance-Driven Giving

In order to start building a giving habit, consider the following:

1. Do you relate to any of the roadblocks to giving we mentioned early in the chapter? Were you able to deal with them? If so, how did you do that?

2. Review the list of fifteen items on our list of suggestions for building a giving habit. Choose three of them and give them a try in the coming week.

3. Have you experienced any of the benefits of giving in the past year? Which ones? How did that make you feel, and did it motivate you to give more?

Four Reasons Not to Give

This whole book has been focused on helping you develop performance-driven giving in your life. Giving can change your life! However, there are times when you should not give. If you are motivated by any of these reasons, check your heart make you're thinking about giving in the right spirit.

1. Don't give to get noticed.

Sometimes in the news you will see a business mogul who makes a flashy presentation of their giving. When you approach giving this way, that is your reward: getting noticed. That is not a healthy reason to give if that's your only motive.

When speaking to the religious leaders of his day, Jesus said, "Beware of practicing your righteousness before other people in order to be seen by them, for then you will have no reward from your Father who is in heaven" (Matthew 6:1). A little further in this passage, he instructed them to give in secret. It is better to not give at all than to give for the purpose of getting attention from others.

2. Don't give because you feel obligated.

Guilt is rarely a good reason to do anything worthwhile, but many people approach giving this way. They feel obligated to volunteer or make a donation to a cause. That's not to say you can't accomplish good things with your giving, because after all, you're still giving. However, you will miss out on the joy that comes with giving from the heart. Make sure you are properly motivated when giving.

3. Don't give to make up for bad habits or mistakes.

Giving does not cancel out negative actions or past mistakes. Good deeds in one area do not erase bad deeds in another area. Just as a husband who brings flowers to his wife to make up for causing an argument, some people believe that generosity will somehow undo some other transgressions. Money has a spiritual component, but it is not a magic eraser that cancels out negative aspects of our lives.

4. Don't give in order to get something back.

Does giving bring blessings into your life? Absolutely. But this is not the *reason* to give. Blessings come in many different forms, and they are not always financial (or perhaps even usually financial). You should give because you want to, not because you want something from another person (or even from God). People can tell when they are being manipulated, so give out of a pure heart that wants to serve others.

A Conversation with Honorée Corder, Strategic Book Coach

When we were considering who to interview for this chapter on building a giving habit, the first person that came to mind was Honorée Corder. She provides group and one-on-one strategic book coaching to business professionals who want to write, publish, and market their books to bestseller status, create a platform, and develop multiple streams of income.

Honorée is also the author of more than fifty books. She partnered with Hal Elrod to expand *The Miracle Morning* book into an entire series that emphasizes key habits to help you win the day. As an authority on habits and mindset, Honorée is the ideal person to enlighten us on the connection between giving and habits.

We began this conversation by exploring some ways that Honorée practices generosity as an entrepreneur and leader.

I have been a Rotarian for twenty-four years. Rotary is a service orga-nization. The motto is "service above self." We have a four-way test we recognize at the beginning of every meeting: (1) Is it the TRUTH? (2) Is it FAIR to all concerned? (3) Will it build GOODWILL and BETTER FRIENDSHIPS? (4) Will it be BENEFICIAL to all concerned?

Those are some pretty clarifying questions, right? They impacted me when I first joined Rotary all those years ago, and they continue to impact me today.

Another way I give is that I'm on the board of Family and Chil-dren's Services. As a former foster kid, I've benefited from their services. Of course, I cannot repay the folks who helped me. So I pay it forward by volunteering with that organization, serving on the board, and giving financial aid to them during the year.

I am also involved with Habitat for Humanity. We did a Habitat build last fall. It was probably the fifteenth house that I helped build. I was on the board of Habitat many years ago and have loved seeing their impact on the community. There is crossover between Habitat and Rotary, since Rotary is like an umbrella organization that sup-ports other organizations.

As you can see, Honorée is active in community service, which we love as giving partners of Habitat for Humanity. In our next question, we explored some ways that Honorée has built specific giving habits into her life.

I give a portion of every dollar that I earn back to organizations that I support. As money comes in, it is allocated, and that is one of my practices.

I also give by saying thank you. I have a daily practice of writing thank-you notes. Some days I write five or ten notes, depending on what's happened. Some days, I just write one.

I meditate before I get out of bed, but the first thing that I do before I engage in writing, reading, affirmations, or anything else is to send a note in the mail to someone just saying, "Hey, thanks for this cool thing that you did." I love doing that. As part of my morning routine, I give gratitude in thoughts, but I also give gratitude in action.

I like to pay for the car behind me at Starbucks. I often ask, "What are they getting? Let me buy it." And then I'm always gone. Sometimes I'll ask, "What happens when someone pays for the car behind them?" And they'll say, "Well, sometimes they keep it going and it goes for ten people" or something like that.

If you have never read the book Seed Money *by John Hoshor, I highly recommend it. He says that you should never pass up an opportunity to give. So I've adopted that philosophy. If you believe in the law of reciprocity, you know that whenever you give money, it will return to you tenfold. So I will not pass a homeless person. I keep ones, fives, and sometimes twenties in my car for that very reason. If I see someone and they are holding a sign, it's not for me to judge. I just give.*

It doesn't come back from that person. The point of giving is not receiving, but I know it comes back.

One of the themes running throughout these interviews is the recognition that giving comes back to you. That's certainly the case in our interview with Honorée. We asked her to elaborate on some ways that giving benefits not just the receiver, but the giver as well.

I believe this: To whom much is given, much is expected. It is my responsibility to give back. Every dollar I give benefits the universe and the world at large. When I get a big bill, I think, "What is this money going to do for the people who receive it?"

Recently, I got a new client and they paid me a large sum, so their money is benefiting us. In the same way, my money is going out and helping others. There is a great sense of satisfaction that comes with knowing you are part of a larger pattern of giving.

Every dollar I spend, every dollar I give is helping someone. You're blessed to be a blessing. So then the blessings come in different ways. It's not always the case where I give money and then money comes back to me. I get a lot of gifts from people, such as a mug or housewarming gift. I'll also get referral fees and discounts.

All of that giving comes back in little magical ways. When I need something, it shows up.

Thanks, Honorée! We are grateful for your example of giving and the creative ways you add value to the world.

You can visit Honorée's website at https://honoreecorder.com. Make sure to check out her excellent book, *You Must Write a Book*, which will teach you how to generously impact the world with your words. To listen to the entire interview, go to PerformanceDrivenThinking.com/Giving or scan the QR code to visit the page.

We also recommend connecting with Honorée on social media:

Facebook: https://www.facebook.com/honoree.corder
LinkedIn: https://www.linkedin.com/in/honoree
Instagram: https://www.instagram.com/honoree
Twitter: https://twitter.com/Honoree

CHAPTER 11

A Framework for Choosing Where to Give

He who serves the most, reaps the most.
—Jim Rohn

If you have ever traveled to another country on a mission trip, you know what it feels like to be surrounded by needs. If you visit an especially poor area, it is impossible to look around and not feel a bit overwhelmed by the poverty and hunger.

Givers often feel this way when deciding where to invest their time, talent, or treasure. With so many needs in the world, how do you choose where to give?

You can't help everyone, but you can help some. We don't want you to feel discouraged by the overwhelming needs out there. That's why it is important to have a framework for choosing where to give. In this chapter, we'll explore the five elements of the HEART framework of giving as well as some practicalities to consider when giving.

The HEART Framework
We are bombarded with opportunities to serve and give today. A few

decades ago, we had a relatively limited number of organizations and non-profits to help. But today, with so many entrepreneurs starting organizations, our opportunities have exploded. You probably know what it is like to get bombarded with phone calls, letters, or emails requesting support.

But it's not only a matter of getting asked to support more causes than we can reasonably help. For givers, it is also a matter of wanting to do the most good in the world. We want to be responsible stewards of our time, influence, and resources. That's why a framework is helpful for taking the guesswork out of these decisions.

Giving is ultimately a heart-related issue. While there is logic and reason involved, it doesn't matter if our heart is not in it. Let's dive into a framework we call the HEART of giving, which will help you make good choices.

The framework consists of five elements:

1. Human
2. Exciting
3. Action-oriented
4. Rewarding
5. Team-based

These five elements will help you decide how and where to give.

1. Giving Must Be HUMAN

Giving is all about people. Of course there are metrics, data, and many other considerations involved in giving. But it's people who give, and it's people who receive the giving. It's ultimately all about people. That's why we suggest giving to organizations and causes that benefit people first and foremost.

For example, at Morgan James Publishing we support Habitat for Humanity. The direct connection to people is obvious (not to mention that the word "human" is literally included in the name of the organization). Habitat builds houses, and it does not get any more human than that.

That's not to say other organizations are not worth supporting. Many different kinds of organizations and causes can benefit people. Some of them are more directly tied to helping people than others. For example, let's say there is a nonprofit organization that conducts polls or gathers data that helps mission organizations make good decisions. Data and numbers are not very exciting to the average person, and it's hard to emotionally connect. Although an organization like that might be performing a critical function, it's hard to get your team or family excited about a cause that is not directly linked to helping people.

(This would be a good time for leaders of organizations to note that if you want to increase support, make sure to highlight how your mission or services benefit people. It may be obvious to you, but it's not always obvious to others.)

As you are making these decisions about whom to support, ask how exactly they help people. Do they help with food? Shelter? Mental or emotional needs? Housing? Family services? Career guidance? There are many ways to help people, and any of these (and many more) are worthwhile causes.

This is human not only from the side of those receiving our giving. Giving must also be human in the sense that it invites and calls out our humanity and a desire to serve others. Can you unite the humans around you to support this cause? Does it speak to your family's, or your team's, natural interests and passions?

2. Giving Must Be EXCITING

When you are faced with a variety of choices where to give, which ones excite you? This may seem like a silly or perhaps even a juvenile question. But it can play a major part in choosing the right places to invest ourselves and our resources.

Let's look at a couple of examples of what it means to be excited. When air molecules get warmer, they start rising. They literally begin moving upward. That is why the upstairs of a house is usually warmer than the downstairs. It is also why a hot-air balloon rises into the sky. Air moves when it gets excited.

Kids are the same way. When a child gets excited about a movie, a birthday, a treat, or playtime, they have a hard time sitting still. An excited kid is one who moves. When something is exciting, it causes you to move, take action, or feel motivated. So when you look at your giving options, which ones feel motivating?

This will not be the same for everyone, because we each connect with different aspects of an opportunity. This is easy to determine if you are choosing as an individual where to give. But if you are making choices as a family, or as a team or organization, you must take other people's preferences into account.

It should be relatively easy to determine what is exciting just based on conversation with people. But what happens when you come across opportunities that sound interesting, but they are not exciting? There could be several reasons why:

- It doesn't align with your vision or values.
- You don't have a personal connection to the organization or cause.
- Part of your family or team simply isn't enthusiastic about it.
- You can't figure out how it makes a difference in people's lives.
- There is no emotional connection.

Excitement can be hard to quantify, because it sounds too emotional. But we encourage you to think carefully about this aspect of giving, because it can make the difference between an opportunity that looks good on paper and one that motivates you to contribute.

3. Giving Must Be ACTION-ORIENTED

This is directly connected to the last point. Your excitement should be a natural outgrowth of your excitement about a giving opportunity.

Giving should be focused on doing something, not just studying or learning about it. Of course, you should always do your homework when thinking about a giving opportunity. But it shouldn't stay there.

Why do we sometimes get stuck in analysis mode when considering where to give? There are a few reasons.

First, when analytical people are in charge of making decisions, they sometimes get lost in the details. It is easier to put off a decision than to make one when you are unsure about which direction to go.

Second, sometimes we simply want to avoid taking action, because it makes us uncomfortable. As humans, we don't naturally like to be stretched. But that is how we grow. There is no growth unless we do something different from what we have always done. Giving is all about taking action. Make sure your goals create action within your team.

Third, we sometimes get stuck in analysis mode because we are perfectionists and are afraid of making the wrong decision. So we put off the decision, hoping that we can gather more information or do more study.

There is rarely an opportunity to make a foolproof decision. There will always be some element of the unknown, especially when we are talking about organizations or causes that are not totally familiar to us. We must get comfortable with making the best decision possible based on the information at hand.

Plus, if later we feel we made a wrong decision, we can always change course and adjust our giving to reflect newer priorities or better information.

We must be oriented toward action and not just toward analysis. If we have chosen our giving recipients directly, we will have a strong connection and be aligned with the purpose.

4. Giving Must Be REWARDING

This element, in a way, summarizes the previous three. When you give your time or resources, do you receive a meaningful reward in return? Considering this does not mean that you are being selfish. It simply means that you recognize the reciprocal nature of giving—you give and you receive. You cannot do one without the other.

In their book *The Go-Giver*, Bob Burg and John David Mann share the Five Laws of Stratosphere Success. The fifth law is the Law of Receptivity: "The key to effective giving is to stay open to receiving." You have to be open to receiving a reward or blessing as a result of your giving. As others have said before, you cannot receive with a closed fist.

What does this mean in relationship to choosing where to give? It doesn't just mean that you should expect to get some kind of significant reward, although that can sometimes happen. It means that you stay open to receiving the blessings that can come as a result. Sometimes these are unexpected and unusual.

A big key to experiencing rewarding giving is the state of your heart. Are you ready to receive? Can you humbly accept the fact that others want to give to you, just as you want to give to them? Are you open to what God wants to show you through giving? Are you ready to take your life to another level because of the power of giving? Those are all examples of rewards that can come through giving.

One aspect of giving that is seldom talked about in relation to receiving a reward is that there is a risk involved in giving. You never know how it's going to turn out, do you? Sometimes you give and get nothing back in return. In fact, sometimes you get something negative back! That's just the way life works.

However, with greater risk comes the potential of greater reward. Those who play the stock market know this. We are not saying that giving is like playing the stock market, but there is a similar principle of the value of taking a risk.

5. Giving Must Be TEAM-BASED

As you can tell throughout this book, we are a big fan of working in teams! Is it absolutely true that "together everyone accomplishes more" when they work as a team. Your goal should be big enough that no one person can do it alone. It should also engage the whole team in a unified direction for giving.

In a previous point, we talked about some people's tendency to over-analyze giving opportunities and endlessly study. In this point we want to give a warning about people who charge ahead with decisions without involving their family or team.

Any good leader will tell you that buy-in takes time. People need time and space to process decisions—some longer than others. It is much easier just to make decisions and move ahead, but you won't have buy-in from your team nearly as much. The team needs to be involved in choosing where and how to give, and they also need to be involved in celebrating the rewards, whatever form those might take.

The role of a leader is to empower their team and lead them to success. Sometimes that involves making tough calls and standing alone in those decisions. But other times it means setting aside your personal preferences and doing what it best for the group. As you lead your team in giving, we encourage you to take time to work through your options and decisions about giving as a team.

You will usually find that team members have great ideas when they feel that they are in a safe environment and that their ideas will be heard. If you always shut people down, they will not want to participate. So make sure to listen and learn, because you will probably get better ideas in the long run.

When it comes to choosing where to give, select places where your team can participate in the giving process. Maybe it's volunteering, feeding the hungry, tutoring kids, raising funds, doing publicity, or something else. Whatever it is, make this team component a major factor in your decisions where to give.

These five elements of the HEART framework are certainly not the only way to decide where to give, but they are a great foundation for reflection and discussion with your family or team.

Practicalities of Giving

Now that we have established a helpful framework for making decisions about your giving, let's take a look at two practical areas related to giving.

1. How to Establish Partnerships

We have carefully chosen the word "partnership" when it comes to establishing relationships with those you are giving to. The reason is that we don't want you to approach this as if you are doing someone a favor. We want to emphasize that you are partners in giving.

Let's assume that the recipient of your giving is an organization of some kind. Once you have worked through the criteria of the HEART framework above, reach out to a contact at the organization if you don't already have one. You can reach out by phone, email, or social media. But before you do that, it's best to establish some type of relationship with them. Social media is a great way to do this. Follow the networking strategies we laid out earlier in the book.

If you have a mutual connection, you can also ask for an introduction. That is a great way to add value to both people. Your friend gets the pleasure of introducing you to their contact, and of course the contact has the benefit of getting to know you, the person who will become a new partner.

When you approach your contact, share why you are interested in working with them and what you have in mind. Don't present your giving as if it is one-sided. You are benefiting also. If you have a company, your team members will greatly benefit from the giving process. Make sure to communicate that this is an equal partnership where both parties will mutually benefit.

It helps to keep in mind that every organization, and every business, both gives and takes. If you have a company, you are giving and taking as well. Customers or clients give you money, and you give them service or products in return. It's an exchange of value where all parties come away richer. It is no different when you are establishing a giving partnership. Everyone gives, and everyone receives.

Once the partnership is established, treat it like you would treat any other valued relationship. Find more ways to partner, add value, do cross-promotions, make introductions and referrals, and so on.

2. How to Set Giving Goals

Much has been written about goal setting. We believe in keeping things simple and flexible. Here are four principles to follow when setting giving goals both in your family and organization.

1. Consult with your team.

In your family setting, this is your spouse and children. You can also involve grandparents, siblings, or others if your family dynamic calls for it. The most important thing is to communicate with your family. Are they on board? Do you share the same vision for giving? Do you feel it's an important part of your growth and learning? If you have some work to do in this area, don't push ahead until you have harmony and alignment.

It's much the same in a business context, except your team consists of those who serve with you. Depending on the size of your organization, this may be everyone or a select handful of people to help with giving decisions. However, make sure people from every level are involved. One of the major reasons employees sometimes feel disenfranchised is that they are left out of decision-making.

Is your team on board? Do they share a vision for giving? Have you shared your heart for giving and why is it important? Don't assume that people know. There's an old saying: "People are down on what they're not up on." If there is a lack of communication, people concoct their own stories and scenarios. This communication step is critical.

2. Discover what aligns with their passion, purpose, and goals.

Most families have never talked about their goals. That's because they don't have any! Does your family have a shared vision for the future? Are you working toward something specific? These kinds of conversations sometimes feel irrelevant in the hectic pace of everyday life. However, they can help set the vision for the future in a clear way that gets everyone excited and on board.

What are the particular things your family is passionate about? Maybe it's serving inner-city people. Maybe it's helping orphans or another specific cause. What gets your spouse and kids excited? Don't dismiss those elements because those are wonderful hooks upon which to hang giving opportunities.

In your organization's context, what aligns with its mission, vision, and values? What kind of giving goals can you set that will help you achieve those? Maybe it has been a while since you have thought about these topics in your business. If so, it's a great time to revisit them and get clarity on why you exist and what you hope to accomplish. This process will not only get you and your team much more excited about the future, but it will help you set giving goals that are more relevant and purposeful.

Don't forget to seek input from people who are not a part of your organization's leadership. Many times, the people on the ground floor have ideas and contacts you don't know about. They will probably not offer ideas unless you ask them. Make sure to seek their ideas and input, emphasizing that all ideas are welcome.

A common leadership mistake is believing that you have all the best ideas. First of all, it's probably not true (sorry to burst your bubble). And second, you'll miss out on tremendous creative ideas if you think this way.

3. Start small and set a stretch goal.

In chapter 9, you learned about the importance of starting small. When you dive into a new initiative feetfirst, there is a greater chance you will fail or give up. Within your family, set a goal that feels like a stretch, but start small. It sounds like those two things are at odds, but hear us out.

Let's say you want to give a certain amount by the end of three months. Your family is on board, but this is the first time you have given regularly. Set a goal that is a doable and makes you feel like you are accomplishing something worthwhile. However, ramp it up so that you are not diving into it all at once. You will be more likely to stick with it that way.

You can take the same approach in your work or team environment. Decide on a goal that feels like a stretch, but ramp up to it. The timeline for an organization may be much longer than with a family because of planning and budgeting, but the principles are the same. When you focus on small wins in an organization, it also helps reduce potential objections from people. People can see the small wins adding up and will see direct proof of why giving is a great initiative.

4. Explore multiple ways to give.

One of the benefits of understanding personality types or love languages is that you realize people love to give and receive in different ways. In your family, it's important to encourage everyone to give in ways that are meaningful to them. If you have an introvert in the family, they may not want to do things that feel socially uncomfortable. However, maybe they are the one to write letters, organize information, or do research.

Likewise, not everyone in an organization values the same types of giving. While everyone might recognize the benefits, they will not all have the same enthusiasm if you only invite people to participate in one type of giving.

To summarize: Giving does not need to be overly complicated or intimidating. In this chapter, we have shared a straightforward HEART framework to help you choose where to give. Giving should be human, exciting, action-oriented, rewarding, and team-based. When you follow this model, you will be able to put into practice Henry Ford's noteworthy perspective on giving: "To do more for the world than the world does for you—that is success."

Keys to Performance-Driven Giving

In order to give in a thoughtful and systematic way, consider the following:

1. Review the five elements of the HEART framework. Which one do you resonate with most, and which one do you resonate with least? Why?
2. Make a list of at least three potential partners in giving. Which of these entities are you most interested in talking to, and how do you envision giving to them? Make a plan to begin following them on social media or scheduling a phone call in the next two weeks.
3. What are the next steps in helping your family or organization establish healthy goals for giving?

A Checklist for Evaluating Giving Opportunities

This checklist uses the HEART framework we discussed above. It can be useful for evaluating various giving opportunities, but is also a summary you can use for reflection or discussion.

1. Human
- Does it benefit people directly?
- How does it benefit people? Food, housing, family services, career, etc.?

- Does it invite you to serve others?
- Does it speak to your family's or team's natural interests and passions?

2. Exciting
- Do you feel motivated or inspired to take action?
- Does it align with your vision or values?
- Are others around you enthusiastic about it?
- Do you feel an emotional connection to the cause or organization?
- Can you clearly see how it makes a difference in people's lives?

3. Action-Oriented
- Does it invite you to grow and stretch?
- Is there a clear call to action by getting involved?
- Is it aligned with your purpose?

4. Rewarding
- Do you embrace the reciprocal nature of giving?
- Are you open to receiving blessings or rewards?
- Are you willing to accept the risk of giving?

5. Team-Based
- Is your family or team involved in choosing?
- Are you empowering your team to get involved?
- Have you asked your family or team for their input?
- Are you truly listening to the people around you?
- How can your family or team be involved in this opportunity?

A Conversation with Janet V. Green, CEO of Habitat for Humanity Peninsula and Greater Williamsburg

Now that you have read about a framework for choosing where to give, we would love to introduce you to Janet V. Green, the leader of Morgan James Publishing's primary giving partner.

Janet has been the CEO of Habitat for Humanity Peninsula and Greater Williamsburg in Newport News, Virginia, since 2002. Habitat for Humanity partners with people to build homes so they can put down roots and build equity. With 1,400 locations in the United States and a presence in nearly a hundred countries around the world, people can get involved with Habitat in many different ways.

Whenever you pick up a Morgan James book, you will the Habitat for Humanity logo on the back, as well as Habitat information on the copyright page. I (David) reached out to Janet in 2006 to see how Morgan James could be helpful, and we have been proud to partner with Habitat ever since.

Before getting involved with Habitat, Janet held numerous other leadership roles. She was also the special assistant to President Bill Clinton and director of White House operations for the first Clinton administration in 1993–1997. You could say she knows a thing or two about leadership, partnerships, and bringing together people for the greater good!

We began our conversation with this simple question: "How does someone get involved and begin giving to Habitat for Humanity? Do they just reach out to their local Habitat and talk to someone?"

It's really just that simple. The great thing about Habitat is that as much as we would love financial support, we also really need volunteers as well as more donations for our ReStore locations. We use volunteers everywhere. All of our homes are constructed by volunteers.

We have a contractor, so we're not looking for somebody who is a good carpenter. We just want people who are willing to be safe and learn on the job site. We teach them everything they need to know to help us build a home. Habitat uses licensed subcontractors for electrical, plumbing, and HVAC. But otherwise, it's volunteers.

If a company wants to get involved, we have team-building days, where they can come and work at a job site. Oftentimes, these experiences lead to a longer and more fulfilling partnership with Habitat. We can even bring them back to the Habitat offices to do facilitation and discuss how they worked together on the job site.

Company team members can also work in our ReStore locations, which I mentioned a moment ago. These stores are nonprofit home improvement centers. We accept donations from everyone. If people would like to be involved with Habitat, but they don't want to be outside working in the elements, they can serve with ReStore. They can price items, set up displays, assist customers, and many other things. One hundred percent of the profits from our ReStore locations stays right here locally to help build more homes.

You can also help Habitat by doing something at your own company. For example, we've had companies host dress-down Jean Day, where everybody contributes $10 and they can dress in jeans. All of that money comes to Habitat. We've had a lot of companies move their headquarters, and they can not only donate office items to us, but also put up a bucket with a sign that says "Put all your change in here for Habitat." So there are a lot of different ways to get involved.

If you've read this far in the book, you know that giving not only helps those who receive your giving; it changes you as well. We were curious how this principle applies to those who help Habitat for Humanity. So we asked Janet how Habitat's giving partners are changed in the process of their giving.

That's one of the more remarkable things. You hear this all the time, but I get to see it up close. People often say, "I got more than I gave." They may be giving to a lot of other wonderful nonprofits, but with Habitat, they can drive by the home twenty or thirty years later, point to it, and say, "I helped build that porch. I helped build that room. I painted that house." You can know with pride that the homeowner who purchased the home is probably still living there.

We have built over two hundred homes. We've only had three foreclosures. Sadly, all were due to the death of the homeowner. One of the families turned the house back to Habitat so we could resell it to another family with low to moderate income.

Our homeowners also know that this is their dream and that they hope to turn this whole house over to their children. Many people have the impression that Habitat gives people these homes, but they're paying a monthly mortgage. It's just a no-interest monthly mortgage for twenty or thirty years.

And David Hancock, being a former mortgage banker, certainly knows that very well. So for a lot of companies that work with us, they're out there one day, they're building the house. They think they're building it with Habitat, but they're really building it with the Smith family. They get to know the family. They get to know the kids. They can point to the home with pride.

We've had one business, Newport News Shipbuilding, which has built eighteen consecutive homes with us. And at each of those groundbreakings and dedications, all the past homeowners come, and the Shipyard volunteers haven't seen the kids maybe for a couple of years. They're now in middle school or high school.

It really is a family that we're building with. We would love for everybody to become involved with Habitat any way they want to.

Thank you, Janet! It is a privilege and honor to partner with you at Morgan James! To listen to the entire interview, go to PerformanceD-rivenThinking.com/Giving or scan the QR code to visit the page.

You can learn more about Habitat for Humanity Peninsula and Greater Williamsburg at https://www.habitatpgw.org. Make sure to connect with Janet and Habitat PGW on social media:

Janet V. Green
LinkedIn: https://www.linkedin.com/in/janet-v-green-66655a5

Habitat for Humanity Peninsula & Greater Williamsburg
Facebook: https://www.facebook.com/HabitatPGW
Instagram: https://www.instagram.com/habitatpgw
Twitter: https://twitter.com/habitatpgw
YouTube: https://www.youtube.com/user/habitatpgw

CHAPTER 12

Embracing the Overflow: Life as a Giver

For it is in giving that we receive.
—Francis of Assisi

Earlier in the book, we referenced a ceremony from the Jewish tradition that uses a saucer, cup, and wine. As the wine is poured into the cup and runs over into the saucer, those present are reminded why it's important to live out of the overflow. There is another wonderful story that shows why it is important to embrace this wonderful life of giving and generosity.

A father gathered a $1 bill and a $10 bill and called his daughter Susie to his side. He said, "Susie, I want to teach you the most important thing about money and God that I can share with you. My father taught this to me when I was as old as you are now, and I think you are old enough to learn an important truth about money. But I am going to need your help. Could you help me?"

Susie, with a wide smile breaking across her face, said, "Sure, Dad!"

"Great, Susie! This is really simple, but sometimes the simplest things to understand are the hardest things to do in life. So, I want you to remember this moment and how God wants you to live with money. Hold out your hand."

Susie held out her hand with curiosity and excitement as her father placed the $1 bill into it. "Susie, this dollar in your hand is pretty nice, right? What are some things you could buy with $1?"

"Well, I could get gum, candy, or small toy at the store!"

Her father chuckled, "Yes, you can think of a lot of things to do with that dollar. Now, I want you to close your hand around the dollar and hold on to it. Now suppose I want to give you this." Her father takes out the $10 bill and asks, "Where can I put it?"

He playfully takes Susie's hand holding on to the $1 bill and puts the $10 on top of her fist. "Susie, I can't give you this $10, because you are holding on to that $1 too tight!"

Susie laughed as her father explained the story. "Here is what my dad taught me and I want to teach you about money: Live open-handed. If you keep your hand open, I can place the $1 in it. I could take it out and put this $10 in it. In fact, I could leave the $1 and place the $10 make it $11. Wouldn't that be fun to take to the store?

"Susie, you must always live with open hands toward God. He can put things into your hand and give you more. But if you hold on to the blessings he puts into your hand and claim them for yourself, he can't give you more."

We hope this book has blessed you on your journey to becoming a performance-driven giver. When you become a giver, you can embrace the overflow and live with open hands, because it's the only pathway to real fulfillment, joy, and meaning.

In order to encourage you in your journey to embrace the overflow, we offer a summary of the book's content as well as an assessment to help you gauge your level of giving.

Twenty-Five Qualities of Givers

These are hallmarks of givers. Strive to develop these qualities in yourself and your family, as well as looking for these qualities in people on your team.

1. Enjoy their work
2. Give personally to others
3. Love the process of giving, not just the outcome
4. Enjoy new challenges and opportunities
5. Are loyal to the organization
6. Are concerned for others
7. Do more than expected
8. Learn continually
9. Focus on goals
10. Have positive relationships with co-workers
11. Have their personal financial life in order
12. Deal with stress in healthy ways
13. Are emotionally healthy
14. Grow spiritually
15. Don't limit themselves to what is comfortable
16. Don't overthink things and take action
17. Are willing to accept constructive feedback
18. Are humble yet confident
19. Listen to other well
20. Volunteer for opportunities
21. Connect people to each other
22. Contribute to a positive culture
23. Have a positive attitude
24. Love to help others succeed
25. Set realistic but attainable goals

Twenty-Five Qualities of Takers

These are hallmarks of takers. Avoid these qualities, because they will prevent you from becoming a performance-driven giver. In addition, try to avoid hiring or serving with people who show an excessive number of these qualities, because they will negatively impact any group.

1. Have a cynical or negative attitude
2. Do not give personally to others
3. Always focus on the outcome, not the process
4. Avoid new challenges and opportunities
5. Sow dissention in the group or organization
6. Gossip about others
7. Do only what is expected and nothing more
8. Don't learn unless they are required to do so
9. Don't set or achieve goals
10. Typically have conflict with co-workers
11. Have messy personal finances
12. Deal with stress in unhealthy ways
13. Are emotionally unhealthy
14. Are spiritually stagnant
15. Are often irritable
16. Avoid people when possible
17. Have no interest in personal growth
18. Avoid anything that makes them uncomfortable
19. Overanalyze everything and rarely take action
20. Don't accept constructive feedback well
21. Are arrogant yet insecure
22. Don't listen to others well
23. Don't volunteer for opportunities
24. Are always concerned about what they will get
25. Rarely think about helping others succeed

Quiz: Are You a Giver or a Taker?

Are you ready for a moment of truth? If you would like to discover whether you are a giver, a taker, or somewhere in between, rate yourself on the following twenty questions. Give yourself a score from 1 (low) to 5 (high) on each question.

1. I personally give my time and money to help others in need. _____

2. I give with a joyful spirit, not because I feel compelled or obligated. _____

3. I am constantly growing through reading, learning, and other personal development. _____

4. I have a positive attitude and outlook. _____

5. I understand the value of serving with a team and enjoy working with others. _____

6. I see myself not as an owner of my possessions, but as a manager whom God has entrusted with resources and opportunities. _____

7. I am growing spiritually through service, Bible reading, church involvement, and prayer. _____

8. I have control over my personal finances; I keep a monthly budget and have low personal debt. _____

9. I am building my personal income through a side business, investments, or other means. _____

10. I maintain positive relationships with friends, family, clients, customers, and colleagues. _____

11. I give to other business or community leaders by making referrals and introductions, and I often promote other people's businesses. _____

12. I genuinely listen to others with empathy and understanding. _____

13. I volunteer for projects in my job or for service in the community or with other organizations. _____

14. I set realistic but attainable goals and see them through. _____

15. I strive to develop new habits that take my personal development to a higher level. _____

16. I usually do more than is expected. _____

17. I love to help other people succeed. _____

18. I plan my personal, family, or business giving in advance. _____

19. I can accept constructive feedback and learn from it without taking it personally. _____

20. I do my best to resolve conflicts with other people quickly. _____

TOTAL POINTS _____

If you scored 1–25 points, you need serious growth as a giver.

Don't be discouraged by the fact that you have a lot of work to do. The vast majority of people fall into this category. But now that you have read this book and are aware of the growth you need, that puts you on a whole new pathway to giving!

Identify the five areas in this quiz where you need to grow, talk to an accountability partner, and develop a plan to work on each of these areas, perhaps one area per week for the next five weeks. Then choose another five areas to work on. Growth as a giver is a lifelong process. Don't give up, start with small wins, and keep moving forward.

If you scored 26–50 points, you are on the right track.

You have some work to do, but you also have some notable strengths. Giving is not a comparison game, but realize that you are doing better than most people. The most important thing right now is to examine your heart and ask why you want to grow. Are you truly motivated to be the best, most effective version of yourself?

Identify the five areas in this quiz where you need to grow, talk to an accountability partner, and develop a plan to work on each of these areas, perhaps one area per week for the next five weeks. Then choose another five areas to work on. Growth as a giver is a lifelong process. Don't give up, start with small wins, and keep moving forward.

If you scored 51–75 points, you are a giver who needs to brush up in a few areas.

You are doing great! You have some areas you need to shore up, but overall you are engaged in a giving life. You have significant strengths that are helping you impact other people at a high level. Your biggest challenge right now will be the temptation to stay at your current level of influence and giving. Do you really want to grow? If so, you'll need to embrace some discomfort. But that's what real leaders do.

Identify three areas in this quiz where you need to grow, talk to an accountability partner who can help you, and develop a plan to work on these areas. Perhaps work on each area for a month to make sure it's completely solid before moving on to the next one. Then repeat as needed.

If you scored 76–100 points, you are a giver who is making a major difference!

Congratulations! You are an amazing giver who is no doubt making a big difference in people's lives. You have a few areas that could use some attention, but overall you are a strong giver who realizes the importance of giving not just in your personal life, but in your family and community also.

A big challenge you will face is becoming complacent. When you are operating near the top of your game, it's difficult sometimes to justify the extra effort only to improve a little bit. But we assure you, it's worth it! You've come this far already. Why not go all the way and become a truly world-class giver?

We suggest that you seek out a mentor who can review your scores and help you identify one or two areas where you can grow and have even more impact. You won't get there alone. You'll need other leaders to come alongside you and show you the way.

Does Your Cup Overflow?

Psalm 23 is perhaps the most famous passage in the Bible. It focuses on the image of God as the great Shepherd of his people. Verse 5 gives a wonderful image of God's provision for his people: "You prepare a table before me in the presence of my enemies; you anoint my head with oil; my cup overflows."

As you consider the state of your life in this moment, would you say that your cup overflows? Do you sense God's blessing in your life? Do you feel you're a channel of those blessings for other people? Do you feel a sense of abundance, overflow, and goodness? Is that what you want for your life?

We hope this book has sparked a deep urgency for you to become a giver. Strangely enough, some people are uncomfortable with this challenge. Why? Because it is different. We are so used to focusing on taking that the whole concept of an overflowing life of giving is completely foreign.

But imagine what can happen if you surrender your life and truly become a giver. You can embrace a whole new identify as one who lives not for themself, but for others. You can experience a joy that is deeper than anything you have felt. And you can impact people now and in future generations in ways you never thought possible.

Jim Rohn said, "Only by giving are you able to receive more than you already have." Are you ready to start giving—and receiving—more?

Keys to Performance-Driven Giving

In order to embrace the overflow, consider the following:

1. Review the list of twenty-five qualities of both givers and takers. Which list describes you the most? (Be honest.)
2. If you did not complete the quiz in this chapter, please do so and follow the instructions for next steps according to your score.
3. Do you sense the overflow in your life? If so, what do you attribute the overflow to? If not, why? What is the missing component?

Five Steps to Performance-Driven Giving

1. Embrace your new identity as a giver.
2. Visualize how you can impact your family, organization, community, and the world through giving.
3. Set giving goals and start small.
4. Find a way to give every day.
5. Take intentional action by joining other performers at www.performancedrivenacademy.com.

A Conversation with Skip Prichard, CEO of OCLC

As we wrap up this chapter, we wanted to interview someone who truly "embraces the overflow" and approaches life from the standpoint of giving. We could think of no one better than Skip Prichard.

Skip is the *Wall Street Journal* bestselling author of *The Book of Mistakes: 9 Secrets to Creating a Successful Future*. He is also the CEO of OCLC, a global nonprofit computer library service and research organization. Skip has run global businesses ranging from the startup phase to mature businesses with over $1.5 billion in revenue. He is a giver in every aspect of his life, including business. In fact, *Harvard Business Review* labeled Prichard as a rare social CEO and a "relentless giver."

Skip shared some thoughts on how leaders can be more intentional in their giving.

> *You must make it part of your routine. You can express it in meetings, write notes, give public praise, and you must be genuinely thrilled to put the spotlight on those who make a difference.*
>
> *Leaders who express gratitude do it best when it is specific, authentic, timely, unexpected, sincere, duplicatable, and personalized. These are the elements of leadership gratitude that make an enormous difference.*
>
> *Imagine hearing this in a meeting: "Susan, you completed this project on time, under budget, and you did it in a way that was innovative. You not only delivered for the organization; you also taught us an entirely new way to operate. Now that you have trailblazed a new way for us to operate, we want to reward you with a new opportunity."*
>
> *Contrast that with generalized statements like "Thank you for your work" and little information as to why something was noticed.*
>
> *Best of all, when delivered with specificity, gratitude teaches the entire organization what matters. It highlights the value of the organization in a tangible way.*

We wanted to find out specific ways that leaders can encourage their team members to become better givers. Skip has plenty of experience in this area. He shared several great tips any leader can put into practice.

> *The first step is to hire people who have the giving qualities already, a nice shortcut. I am fortunate to find people who want to make an impact.*
>
> *Beyond that, model the way. If the leader is passionate about personal growth, many in the organization will take up the cause. Once they do, they rarely give it up because the benefits are extraordinary. Jim Rohn shared advice with me once long ago to "Work harder on*

yourself than you do on your job." It was the best advice I ever received, and I share it with all the organizations I have the privilege to lead.

If you work hard on you, everyone benefits. It's counterintuitive to the advice that you should work hard on your projects, or what your boss says is the most important. Instead, work on personal growth. Give naturally and joyfully. Let leaders on the team lead from their strengths.

Giving doesn't only help the organization. It is also a major force that helps the leader to be stronger as well. We asked Skip how giving helps motivate us to achieve our goals.

There's plenty of hard research to back up the claim that gratitude improves performance, but in the end, I still find it a bit mysterious. When the right person serves it up at the right time and in the right way, it fuels success.

Giving and receiving are linked. When you give, you will find it easier to receive. That allows new opportunities to be planted. When you practice gratitude, you will find that others are magnetized to your own cause. They will naturally come alongside you to guide, assist, and help you achieve what you could never have done on your own.

Skip elaborated on this last point and shared how giving had personally impacted him. You'll love the story he shares about his childhood!

Growth is important to me in every way. Growth encompasses personal and team growth, the expansion of potential. When that happens, business metrics like revenue growth will happen.

Giving stems from the unique way I grew up. My parents took in the abandoned, the addicted, and the abused. Some would stay a night and many for years. I learned the art of pouring into others by watching them.

My mom was an amazing counselor and motivator who touched every person she encountered. I was the beneficiary of this amazing childhood, and I am motivated to be a fraction of that for others. There is nothing more gratifying that watching someone reach their goals and exceed what they thought was possible.

Finally, we asked Skip to share some details about OCLC's giving partnerships and the impact they have on the community.

OCLC is a consistent winner of regional and national Best Place to Work awards. The organization's innovative technology platforms, high employee engagement, and superior benefits are often cited as attraction and retention drivers for its staff. A commitment to advancing racial equity and fostering sustainable development goals among its members are important values for customers, members, and associates.

Among OCLC's inventive programs are opportunities for peer-to-peer recognition called You Rock, invitations for customers to recognize staff members, and its award-winning wellness initiatives.

A commitment to furthering access to information for global libraries speaks to the heart of academia, learning, and open information. OCLC provides free research, training, and advocacy services for libraries and archives. The organization also partners with local community organizations through its volunteer We Care program, Diversity Council memberships, and employee-led charitable campaigns. Corporately, OCLC sponsors a number of industry events, conferences, and awards focused on leading libraries and librarians.

As the president and CEO, I can say with confidence that the spirit of giving at OCLC is not a corporate initiative but comes from a truly generous spirit of employees who are always thinking of others first.

Thanks, Skip! We appreciate your spirit of generosity and the example you continue to set in giving.

You can check out Skip's website at https://skipprichard.com. We also recommend checking out Skip's amazing book, *The Book of Mistakes*. To listen to the entire interview, go to PerformanceDrivenThinking.com/Giving or scan the QR code to visit the page.

We also recommend connecting with Skip on social media:

Facebook: https://www.facebook.com/SkipPrichardCEO
LinkedIn: https://www.linkedin.com/in/skipprichard
Instagram: https://www.instagram.com/skipprichard
Twitter: https://twitter.com/skipprichard
Podcast: https://www.skipprichard.com/podcast

Conclusion:

One Hundred Years from Now

Happiness doesn't result from what we get, but from what we give.
—Ben Carson

One of most popular Christmas stories ever written is *A Christmas Carol* by Charles Dickens. In the story, the miserly businessman Ebenezer Scrooge has the opportunity to see his past, present, and future when he is visited by three spirits. He sees the sins and regrets of his past, the heartbreaking reality of the present for Bob Cratchit and his family, and a dire future for the Cratchits—and himself—if the future does not remain unchanged.

What if you were given an opportunity like Ebenezer Scrooge? What if you could be magically transported to see what the outcome of your life would be? Except we're not going to the near future. We're visiting one hundred years from now.

You are your children have passed from this life, as well as most of your grandchildren. Those who carry your family name and legacy are your great-grandchildren and their descendants. What will they know about you? What will their lives be like? What kind of world will you have helped them create?

Those are impossible questions to answer from the vantage point of today. However, it's fun to think about their lives and how you could change them radically by your giving today. And not just the lives of your descendants, but the lives of people all over the world.

Throughout this book, we have given you many stories and images related to giving. But the metaphor we keep coming back to is a tree. Why? Because a tree best represents how giving starts small, branches out to impact others, and bears fruit not only in the present but in the long-term future as well. A mighty oak tree begins as a tiny acorn, but over the decades it becomes strong and sturdy.

Dave Ramsey is famous for saying, "If you will live like no one else, later you can live like no one else." This is especially true when you embrace a time frame that is much bigger: one hundred years from now. Except it won't be you that is living like no one else. It will be generations of your family who come after you, in addition to all the lives you were able to impact by giving.

We often talk about the need to create a better world, a better future. But it begins with the here and now. It begins with the growth you can experience if you are willing to get a little bit uncomfortable. A tiny acorn has to let go of its current form if it wants to become a mighty oak. We challenge you to embrace growth and change so you can become something greater later on.

Do you want to make a difference? Of course you do. We all do. But if you want to receive all the blessings of giving both now and in the future, you must embrace the life of a giver today.

In the movie *The Shawshank Redemption*, Tim Robbins plays Andy, a prison inmate who has been wrongly convicted of murdering his wife. He has dreams of escaping prison and heading to Mexico. In one of the movie's most gripping scenes, he whispers to his friend Red: "Get busy living, or get busy dying."

Throughout this book, we have emphasized the need to embrace a life of giving. It's not a one-time action. It's a lifestyle, a mindset, an attitude. If giving equals living, then perhaps we should get busy giving, or get busy dying.

We encourage you to get busy giving and not waste one more moment. Are you ready to impact the world with a life that is fully open to giving?

A Conversation with Rita Ralston, Executive Director at Ronald McDonald House Charities of Charlottesville, Inc., and Charles George, Marketing Expert and Copywriter

We wanted to close out the book with a special conversation that embodies everything we have talked about in the book. We are thrilled to introduce you to Rita Ralston, who leads the Ronald McDonald House (RMHC) in Charlottesville, Virginia, and Charles George, whose was able to stay at this RMHC location when his son was critically ill a few years ago.

The Ronald McDonald House of Charlottesville exists to serve and sustain families when serious illness or injury strikes the most cherished part of their lives, their children. It is currently in its forty-first year of providing a temporary home away from home for families whose children are receiving treatment for a serious illness or injury in Charlottesville. In an effort to lessen the burden, reduce stress, keep the family intact, and enhance the quality of life for these families, they provide affordable housing in a caring home-like atmosphere.

Through Charles's and his family's stay at RMHC a few years ago, he and Rita developed a friendship and mutual respect, out of which was born the *Walking with Families* podcast, which you can access at the link at the end of the interview. This comes from a phrase Rita uses with families as they leave: "Remember, we are always walking with you."

We began the conversation by asking Rita to share why serving with RMHC was such a meaningful role.

> *Oh gosh, that's a hard one, because there really are so many things that make your heart smile, such as getting to know parents over the time they're here. You develop a special relationship to them.*
>
> *I also love hearing from parents afterwards. The experience of staying with us during a difficult time is just huge. I love seeing the children and getting employees committed to the mission.*

We followed up by asking Rita about some of the ways she has seen giving impact the person who is making a donation or contributing to the mission of RMHC.

> *I love the idea of transformational giving, which comes from the author Kay Sprinkel Grace. Whenever someone gives, they are transformed. We have some folks who have given us hugely generous gifts. That is marvelous, and those kinds of gifts clearly keep us going.*
>
> *But to see the folks who give their best gift, which may be $5 or $10, that's really special to me. It is so inspiring to see people reach outside themselves, turn the binoculars from looking at themselves to the outside, and give something meaningful. If your best gift is $5 and you've given it to RMHC, I am over the moon.*

One of the many people Rita and RHM Charlottesville has impacted is Charles George. We asked Charles to share his story.

> *My wife was in the hospital on bed rest for the last six weeks of her pregnancy. We found out that our son had congenital heart disease before he was born, and my wife was dealing with health issues as well. We were transferred from a hospital in Richmond to the Univer-*

sity of Virginia Medical Center. We were there for three weeks prior to his birth.

We knew our son needed heart surgeries, and that we were going to be at the hospital a long time. My wife was experiencing all the things that happens when you have a child, plus all the additional stress that comes with a newborn who has serious medical issues.

The UVA staff came to us and said, "You guys can get a hotel, but there's another place called the Ronald McDonald House across the street. We think the two of you would really enjoy going there, if you're open to it." I had heard of RMHC but didn't know much about it.

For eight months out of Thomas's first year of life, he endured two heart surgeries and two other life-saving operations. I had never experienced this level of stress. Our entire lives quickly found a new normal. Our careers, home life, daily routines, and every other aspect of our lives were disrupted.

Our new routine consisted of (1) spending countless days, weeks, and months in the hospital, over an hour away from our home, as Thomas fought for his life; and (2) staying at our "home away from home," the Ronald McDonald House of Charlottesville.

When nothing seemed normal, we knew RMHC had a home-cooked meal each night, a bed to sleep in, a warm shower, and a support group of other families going through similar challenges. The connection with other families would have been lost if we were staying in a hotel.

After Thomas came home from the hospital, we had another heart surgery to go through, plus other additional visits to RMHC. One time we dropped by to visit, and Rita mentioned she loved seeing the kids come back. After that, we made a point to pay Rita a visit every time Thomas had an appointment.

One day we brought Thomas by to see Rita. She had just gotten a pair of Ronald McDonald shoes the day before. Thomas was the first one to wear them. One of my favorite pictures shows him sitting on the *steps of RMHC, laughing and wearing those huge shoes. Rita's love and dedication for all the families there made such a big difference.*

When Thomas turned three years old, he faced his third heart surgery. My son did not survive the complications from this heart surgery. This was the most devastating moment of my life. The weeks and months that followed were my lowest moments. The stress and pain were unbelievable.

As a result, I started to study how families dealt with losing a child. I learned that giving back was an important way to process the grief and heal. A couple of months after we lost Thomas, Rita and I started a podcast to help families. This of course led to the Walking with Families *podcast.*

Over the years, Rita has been like a second mother, and we have continued to maintain our friendship. I will always be grateful to her and RMHC for being there for our family when we needed it most.

Thanks, Rita and Charles! We appreciate you sharing how the Ronald McDonald House can make a huge impact in family's lives. To listen to the entire interview, go to PerformanceDrivenThinking.com/Giving or scan the QR code to visit the page.

You can find out more about the Ronald McDonald House of Charlottesville by visiting https://rmhcharlottesville.org. You can also discover more about Charles's services by visiting https://charlesgeorge.com.

Make sure to connect with Rita, Charles, and RMHC of Charlottesville on social media:

Rita Ralston:
LinkedIn: https://www.linkedin.com/in/rita-ralston-15472226

Charles George:
Facebook: https://www.facebook.com/1charlesgeorge
LinkedIn: https://www.linkedin.com/in/charlesgeorge

Ronald McDonald House of Charlottesville:
Facebook: https://www.facebook.com/RMHCCharlottesville
Twitter: https://twitter.com/RMHofCville
YouTube: https://www.youtube.com/channel/
UCk4RkJ2n75qJ_BhcIRymdUw
Instagram: http://instagram.com/rmhofcville

Walking with Families Podcast:
https://podcasts.apple.com/us/podcast/walking-with-families-podcast-hope-inspiration-weekly/id1190713907

Acknowledgments

As we continue on our journey of performance, we realize that without the help of top performers, this dream would not have become a reality. We would sincerely like to express our great appreciation to the following individuals for their valued support and Performance-Driven attitude in helping us bring this project to completion:

Jim Howard, our publisher
Margo Toulouse, Author Relations Manager
Amanda Rooker, our editor
Brittany Douglas, for our cover concept and branding
Chris Treccani, for our cover, interior design, and layout
Bethany Marshall, who pitches us to the bookstores
Nickcole Watkins, Amber Parrott, Taylor Chaffer, Lauren Howard, Heidi Nickerson, and Jessica Moran, our author support, marketing, and publicity team
Kent Sanders, our esteemed wordsmith

We would also both like to thank our families and individual friends who throughout our lives have enabled us to pursue the performance of a lifetime.

Most importantly, we want to thank those who read this book and use it.

Performance-Driven Resources

Download the *Performance-Driven Giving* supplementary material from

PerformanceDrivenThinking.com/Giving

You will get access to the full interviews of the people featured in the book, plus additional bonuses that will enhance your performance driven journey.

PERFORMANCE-DRIVEN MASTERMIND

A mastermind facilitated by Morgan James Publishing founder, David Hancock, along with Bobby Kipper that focuses on proven Performance-Driven Thinking strategies!

Here is what is included:

- Two ninety-minute calls each month
- Cover the entire arsenal of Performance-Driven tactics so you achieve results faster
- Three specific ways to measure success in life and business
- Strategies to perform at your highest level
- Minimum one live group event each year
- Limited availability to ensure interaction with each member

Learn more about the Performance-Driven Mastermind by visiting www.PerformanceDrivenMastermind.com

PERFORMANCE-DRIVEN ACADEMY

Take your performance to the next level by becoming a member of the Performance-Driven Academy!

Each month, we will explore *Performance-Driven Thinking* at a much deeper level through specialized classes, tutorials, and actionable lessons. Our goal is to help you achieve your best performance and have greater impact.

Members Benefit From:

- Weekly Exclusive Performance Tips
- Performance-Driven Coaching Videos
- Exclusive Audio Updates
- Live Q&A Sessions with the Authors
- Discounts to Performance-Driven Events

Learn more about the Performance-Driven Academy by visiting
www.PerformanceDrivenAcademy.com

WE WOULD LOVE
TO HEAR FROM YOU

We would love to hear from you.

We would enjoy hearing your thoughts, ideas, and inspiration on how the book impacted you and your life.

Please reach out to us and share your story at

www.PerformanceDrivenThinking.com/Story

ABOUT THE AUTHORS

David Hancock is a *Wall Street Journal* and *USA Today* bestselling author, the co-founder of Performance-Driven Thinking™, and the founder of Morgan James Publishing. NASDAQ cites David as one of the world's most prestigious business leaders, and he is reported to be the future of publishing. As founder of Morgan James Publishing, David was also selected for *Fast Company* magazine's Fast 50 for his leadership, creative thinking, significant accomplishments, and significant impact on the industry over the next ten years.

David also serves as president of the executive board for Habitat for Humanity Peninsula and Greater Williamsburg, and chairman of the board of the National Center for the Prevention of Community Violence.

Bobby Kipper is a *Wall Street Journal* and *USA Today* bestselling author, speaker, and coach, and the co-founder of Performance-Driven Thinking™. He has spent over thirty years providing leadership development, training, and coaching to both the government and private sectors. Bobby believes that we were "born to perform," and his motivational style of speaking and coaching has taken thousands to their best performance to date.

In addition, Bobby is the director of the National Center for the Prevention of Community Violence and is passionate about quality of life and human rights issues for all Americans. His programs to prevent and reduce violence have been featured by the White House, Congress, and thirty-five states across America.

Kent Sanders is a writer who helps leaders grow their business and impact through books and other content. As a former pastor and college professor, he has spent over twenty-five years writing, teaching, and coaching others with a focus on creating high-value content. Kent is also an author coach and host of the *Daily Writer Podcast*, which helps writers cultivate habits for creative success.

A free ebook edition is available with the purchase of this book.

To claim your free ebook edition:

1. Visit MorganJamesBOGO.com
2. Sign your name CLEARLY in the space
3. Complete the form and submit a photo of the entire copyright page
4. You or your friend can download the ebook to your preferred device

Morgan James
BOGO™

A **FREE** ebook edition is available for you or a friend with the purchase of this print book.

CLEARLY SIGN YOUR NAME ABOVE

Instructions to claim your free ebook edition:
1. Visit MorganJamesBOGO.com
2. Sign your name CLEARLY in the space above
3. Complete the form and submit a photo of this entire page
4. You or your friend can download the ebook to your preferred device

Print & Digital Together Forever.

Snap a photo

Free ebook

Read anywhere

CPSIA information can be obtained
at www.ICGtesting.com
Printed in the USA
JSHW022158180422
25057JS00004B/6